The Palgrave Lacan Series

Series Editors
Calum Neill
Edinburgh Napier University
Edinburgh, UK

Derek Hook
Duquesne University
Pittsburgh, USA

Jacques Lacan is one of the most important and influential thinkers of the 20th century. The reach of this influence continues to grow as we settle into the 21st century, the resonance of Lacan's thought arguably only beginning now to be properly felt, both in terms of its application to clinical matters and in its application to a range of human activities and interests. The Palgrave Lacan Series is a book series for the best new writing in the Lacanian field, giving voice to the leading writers of a new generation of Lacanian thought. The series will comprise original monographs and thematic, multi-authored collections. The books in the series will explore aspects of Lacan's theory from new perspectives and with original insights. There will be books focused on particular areas of or issues in clinical work. There will be books focused on applying Lacanian theory to areas and issues beyond the clinic, to matters of society, politics, the arts and culture. Each book, whatever its particular concern, will work to expand our understanding of Lacan's theory and its value in the 21st century.

Thomas Svolos

Culture and Politics on the Couch

Lacanian Interventions

palgrave
macmillan

Thomas Svolos
School of Medicine
Creighton University
Omaha, NE, USA

ISSN 2946-4196 ISSN 2946-420X (electronic)
The Palgrave Lacan Series
ISBN 978-3-031-61364-7 ISBN 978-3-031-61365-4 (eBook)
https://doi.org/10.1007/978-3-031-61365-4

This Palgrave Macmillan imprint is published by the registered company Springer Nature Switzerland AG.
The registered company address is: Gewerbestrasse 11, 6330 Cham, Switzerland

For Fredric Jameson, my teacher

Preface

This book is a wager, a wager that a psychoanalyst—one without specialized training or expertise in political science, sociology, or cultural studies—might have something valuable to contribute to the debates and discussions of political, social, and cultural affairs. There are many books by philosophers and theorists about political and social matters that draw on psychoanalytic theory, but few by psychoanalysts, which is what I present here. I will lay my cards on the table in this preface to make a few tentative proposals about what that might be, all the while knowing that it will only be after the reader has completed the book that they might be willing to respond whether the wager was won.

My assertion is that the particular psychoanalytic contribution to these debates has to do with a dimension of the human experience that is usually opaque to our observations and elucidations—that which Sigmund Freud and Jacques Lacan called, at different points in their work, desire or libido or—to use a French term now adopted without translation globally—jouissance. (Perhaps the only English translation of jouissance that I would consider using is "satisfactioning," a neologism brought to us by Elvis Presley. The non-finite, passive, and even unsubjectified gerund captures some of what Lacan was getting at in French with his use of jouissance.[1])

Much of the accumulated knowledge about politics, society, and culture from those dedicated to its study is based on phenomena transparent to the experts in those fields—observations that might be verifiable, even experiments that can be reproduced, and hypotheses that can be tested and that fall under the rubric of scientific knowledge as defined by Karl Popper.

Psychoanalysts, on the other hand, work in a different realm. Of course, the patients who come to talk with us speak of the knowable events of their lives—their history, the affairs of their day-to-day existence, their relationships, and their work experiences, as well as their experiences of suffering in one form or another. But the psychoanalyst is always on the lookout for something not readily transparent to the observations of the patient, something opaque, something bizarre even, something that is part of the experience of the patient that they are not conscious of, what Freud identified as the unconscious.

The unconscious is a hypothesis of sorts as well, but not a Popperian hypothesis that can be verified or falsified. It is, rather, something that we suppose based on its effects. Through the experience of psychoanalysis, something of the unconscious may be brought into consciousness, but there are other parts that we might only catch a glimpse of, without being able to fully grasp them as objects in our hands, amenable to our willful manipulations.

This unconscious is the realm where desire, libido, and jouissance reside for the speaking being.

My wager, with this book, is that by taking account, in one way or another, of desire, libido, and jouissance, we might find another dimension to political, social, and cultural matters, a dimension that is present, but generally opaque, to those who deal with them.

Let me add one comment about the form of the book. People—patients—present to the psychoanalyst with urgent issues that they wish

[1] "A little less conversation, a little more action, please. All this aggravation ain't satisfactioning me." Lyrics, Elvis Presley, "A Little Less Conversation," accessed on Google lyrics search on January 16, 2024.

to address in their lives. Even in working over an extended period of time with one patient, the analyst is confronted with different situations and demands linked to all the varieties of the ways in which people experience their suffering and the different situations of their lives. That is no less true, in an analogous way, to the varied psychoanalytic interventions on social and political matters that I am providing in this book. Different invitations and demands were presented to me, and the wandering nature of the themes addressed in this book reflects either different demands for me to speak on one topic or another or responses I made as a psychoanalyst to what was happening in the world around me, in my effort to take account of our times. At the beginning of each section or chapter, I will offer a few words of context to set the stage for each of the texts.

I do want to add one comment about the texts in Part II—a lecture in Miami—and Part III—presentations for a Reading Seminar hosted by the Irish Circle of the Lacanian Orientation. Both of these engagements were enriched by the comments and questions of the audience and, in the case of the reading seminar, other reading seminar participants. Their contributions add substantially to the value of the text, and I am grateful to them for allowing the incorporation of their comments in this book.

Omaha, NE, USA
December 2023

Thomas Svolos

[illegible]

Acknowledgements

"History and the Link of the Analytic Act with Civilization" was first published in English in the e-journal *Lacanian Review Online*, #324, on January 12, 2022. This text was first published in Portuguese as "História e a conexão do ato analítico com a civilização" in *Boletim Travessias* [electronic journal of the Escola Brasileira de Psicanálise], #5, on October 27, 2021.

"Psychoanalysis, Science Fiction, and Climate Change" first appeared in English in *Lacanian Review Online*, #336, on April 13, 2022. This text was first published in Catalan as "Psicoanàlisi, ciència ficció i canvi climàtic" on the website *Ciutat de les Lletres* on March 13, 2022.

The following texts were first published in *Lacanian Review Online*:

- "The Unconscious in Play in Voting Today" published as "You're Not in the 1%, so Why Vote Like You Are?" *Lacanian Review Online*, #57, December 4, 2016
- "Bury the Hatchet," *Lacanian Review Online*, #106, November 22, 2018
- "Signifiers of Race Matter" as "Signifiers Matter," *Lacanian Review Online*, #257, July 8, 2020
- "'The Boss' and Psychoanalysis," *Lacanian Review Online*, #84, August 27, 2018

Contents

Part I

Introductory Remarks on Psychoanalytic Interpretation

In this introductory chapter, I wish to take account of the various ways in which scholars "use" Lacanian psychoanalysis in their work. In my approach, which is developed based on two Lacanian constructs—the four discourses elaborated in Seminar XVII *and a distinction between savoir and connaissance developed in* Radiophonie*—I articulate a distinction between what I define as two very different ways of using psychoanalysis in the interpretation of social, political, and cultural phenomena. In as much as the bulk of this text consists of specific psychoanalytic interpretations of different social, political, and cultural phenomena, the introductory and also the concluding remarks are my attempt to develop a theory, as it were, of the distinction of my approach as a psychoanalyst.*

For a more general reader less interested in these theoretical topics or less familiar with the language of Lacanian psychoanalysis and critical theory, the first and last chapter might be skipped.

1

Interpretation in the Discourse of the Psychoanalyst and the Discourse of the University

Abstract From its beginning with the work of Sigmund Freud, the practice and theories of psychoanalysis have attracted interest from a diverse set of scholars who wish to use psychoanalysis in their work. Fredric Jameson and Slavoj Zizek—in distinctive ways—use psychoanalysis as part of a broader dialectical approach to their interpretive strategies for cultural and social criticism. From a Lacanian perspective, this use can be articulated as an instance of the Discourse of the University, in which knowledge acts on the object of the study. Thomas Svolos presents an alternative approach to cultural and social criticism, where the libido or jouissance at stake drives the production of critical discourse—the Discourse of the Analyst. The distinction, however, is a function of the relative position of elements within the discourse and not a value judgement on the preference of one or the other. The Discourse of the University and the Discourse of the Analyst also place emphasis on different aspects of knowledge—imaginary knowledge versus knowledge in the real.

Keywords Discourse of the University • Discourse of the Analyst • Fredric Jameson • Slavoj Zizek • Dialectical criticism • Psychoanalysis in critical theory

T. Svolos, *Culture and Politics on the Couch*, The Palgrave Lacan Series,
https://doi.org/10.1007/978-3-031-61365-4_1

This wager that I am making, that a psychoanalyst may have something valuable to say about political, social, and cultural matters, is a bet that I make based on my experience as an analyst and in my engagement with psychoanalysis.

As a way of introducing this project, I want to take some time to speak to my experience of others, other scholars engaged in similar, related, projects, with the intent of situating the approach that I take here in the context of a field in which others have worked, a field in which others have used psychoanalysis in the interpretation of political, social, and cultural objects.

Let me start with a reference to the work of Fredric Jameson, with particular attention to one of his most comprehensive statements on the act of interpretation: the first chapter in *The Political Unconscious*, titled "On Interpretation: Literature as a Socially Symbolic Act."[1] Jameson's approach here is to prioritize the dialectic, in particular the Marxist dialectic, as the ultimate horizon from which one might provide an interpretation of a piece of literature. While giving plenty of credit to the value of other interpretive models, such as psychoanalysis, Jameson argues that it is the dialectic that provides the ultimate frame of reference, and, in that sense, incorporates into the dialectic all non-totalizing theories that have their own partial zones of validity, such as psychoanalysis. There is an interesting dimension of his approach for the psychoanalyst, namely the reliance on some aspects of Althusserian Marxism as a way in which to configure different levels of causality and organize the relationship among different dimensions of the social totality, such as culture and politics and economic phenomena. The beauty and power of Jameson's dialectical method becomes the way in which he is able to mobilize knowledge of many types in his interpretive approach to individual texts, absorbing into the theoretical apparatus Marxism, psychoanalysis, sociology, literary theory, medieval religious interpretive practices, linguistics, and many other forms of knowledge. This approach is characterized by an explicit defense of totalizing theory and is manifested in the exceptionally rich dialectical deployment that characterizes Jameson's work, as well as the

[1] Fredric Jameson, *The Political Unconscious: Narrative as a Socially Symbolic Act*, Ithaca, Cornell University Press, 1984, pages 17–102.

equally diverse range of theoretical content that informs his interpretations.

In this approach, as I said, psychoanalysis—while very well read and admired by Jameson—is a more local, interpretive code or model that subsequently is subsumed into the larger totalizing theory.

There are some similarities between the approach taken by Fredric Jameson and that by another major figure in cultural studies, Slavoj Zizek. The philosophical reference points are fairly similar. The cultural objects of study, for both of them, are variable and wide reaching. Jameson's background in literary studies is evident in the greater attention to and comprehensiveness of his approach to the novel (and notably in the elucidation of periodization of that literary form into realism, modernism, and postmodernism that aligns with three moments of capitalism), while Zizek leans a bit more on contemporary popular culture (and jokes) as objects for his interpretation. Perhaps the other feature is a more evident and explicit embrace and explication of Lacanian psychoanalytic concepts in Zizek's work.[2]

Putting the points of difference between Jameson and Zizek aside, my assertion is that the dialectical practice of both represent a deployment of knowledge, with knowledge in the position of agent, acting on an object, whatever that object of interpretation might be: a text, a movie, or some political phenomenon. In this sense, the active party in the discourse is knowledge itself acting on the object. The object will get situated, ordered, and configured by the agency of knowledge acting on it. In this sense, what is hidden within the practice is the role of the master, of totality as master, ordering the object of interpretation and classifying it. This aspect of ordering and organizing on the part of a master is the very theme of Empire that I will take up later in the chapter on the Empire of Images.[3] In this mode of interpretation, for example, a novel may end up ordered and re-written in the context of the class relations that are deployed in an analysis of its content and its form. Or, the possibilities, for example, of

[2] See, for that matter, another introduction, the "Introduction" in Zizek's first book (Slavoj Zizek, *The Sublime Object of Ideology*, London, Verso, 1989, pages 1–7) for Zizek's program for a different approach to the relation of dialectics (here, Hegelian as much as Marxist) and psychoanalysis.

[3] See chapter 5 below.

what can be said and what cannot be said in a given text will be found to be limited by the modes of production of a given moment.

This is an enormously powerful approach to interpretation and one which I do not wish to discredit in any way. But, the wager that I wish to make is that psychoanalysis is not only an interpretive code that might be subsumed within some larger totalizing interpretive system. Rather, my fundamental assertion is that psychoanalytic interpretation in the discourse of psychoanalysis is distinctive.

In the approach of Jameson or Zizek, which I will now rewrite in Lacan's notion of the Discourse of the University developed in *Seminar XVII*, psychoanalysis is used as an interpretive code and is subsumed in the greater dialectic. That dialectic can thus be placed in the position of knowledge as agent in the Discourse of the University (acting on the object interpreted).[4] However, in the Discourse of the Analyst, the use of psychoanalysis changes. In the Discourse of the Analyst, the agent in play driving the discourse is not knowledge, but libido or jouissance.[5] A psychoanalytic approach to a political, social, or cultural phenomenon is an attempt to find the libido at stake in the matter—to put the libido in the place of agent acting on the subjectivity or suffering present in the interpreted subject. Even, one might say, present in the political, social, or cultural issue at stake. What is the suffering, what is the libido active in the suffering at play in political conflict or issues around immigration or even the suffering in the story of the autobiography of Bruce Springsteen? These are the questions and the orientation that drove the varied interventions I describe in this book. In this approach, the agent in the discourse is the libido itself acting on the subject and the suffering, which produces the interpretation offered. Knowledge is not absent in the psychoanalytic approach, but in distinction to dialectics in the Discourse of the University, where it is the actual agent, in the psychoanalytic approach, it is the libido itself that serves as the agent. Indeed, in the Discourse of

---

[4] The formulations of the Discourse of the University and Discourse of the Analyst (as well as Discourse of the Master and Discourse of the Hysteric) are developed by Jacques Lacan most comprehensively in Jacques Lacan, *The Seminar of Jacques Lacan: Book XVII: The Other Side of Psychoanalysis (1969–1970)*, New York, Norton, 2007.

[5] For a more comprehensive approach to this agency of the libido, see Thomas Svolos, *The Aims of Analysis: Miami Seminar on the Late Lacan*, New York, Midden Press, 2020.

the Analyst, knowledge is placed in the discursive position of truth, while the master signifier is in the position of truth in the Discourse of the University (as I alluded to in the reference to Empire).

I want to make several other comments that may also articulate other issues at play in the distinction I am trying to articulate between my interpretive use of psychoanalysis and that of others.

The first thing I want to note is that psychoanalysis always begins with the demand, a demand from a patient for some interpretation on the part of the analyst to address some suffering. The object to be worked on is the subject and the suffering of the subject. Like psychoanalysis in its clinical practice, most of the texts included here also began with a demand: a demand to address some form of subjective suffering present on a social level. In many of the cases, a colleague would ask me to comment on something happening in the world around us. If we take into account Lacan's comment, quoted later in the book, that the psychoanalyst must meet the horizon of subjectivity of their time, that is indeed exactly it.[6] In that encounter, the psychoanalyst is always scanning for the libido, or the jouissance, not necessarily evident, but that which is the real agent of the work in interpretation, in elaborating some interpretive production about this encounter.

A notable feature of the distinction between this psychoanalytic discourse and the dialectical approach is that the deployment of knowledge as agent to address an object is frequently marked by an exuberance to say more and more about the object. I will draw from a remark of Jacques-Alain Miller about psychoanalysis itself to note that this approach takes the form of *amplification*: incorporating more and more and more knowledge in the approach to the object.[7] The totality of knowledge is brought into play in the confrontation with the object. Amplification, as Miller has pointed out, is certainly a feature of psychoanalytic work. And, indeed, in the beginning of many clinical psychoanalytic experiences, there is an attempt of the patient to say more and more about their suffering. Knowledge is the driver here too, but the hidden truth is the

[6] See Jacques Lacan, "The Function and Field of Speech and Language in Psychoanalysis," *Écrits: The First Complete Edition in English*, New York, Norton, 2006, page 264, quoted in the introductory remarks to Part IV below.

[7] See Jacques-Alain Miller, *Analysis Laid Bare*, New York, Lacanian Press, 2023.

imperative to master and organize the suffering—it is the Discourse of the University with the master signifier (to name and master the suffering) in the position of the truth of the discourse in this situation. But, in the analytic experience, there is also what Miller has referred to as *reduction*, the identification of a fundamental logic linked to the libido that is essential in the psychoanalytic experience, especially at the end of the work with the psychoanalyst. With this binary in mind, one finds that psychoanalytic interpretations in the Discourse of the Analyst tend to be reduced, simple even, in their attempt to grasp something of the singular libido at play. And, that is true to the style of what I have to say on the varied subjects that I address through this text—these tend to be short interventions in which I attempt to capture the libidinal logic in play.

I want to open a sidebar here and say something about the Discourse of the University and the university itself. Some of my psychoanalyst colleagues can be critical of universities. In part, I think that this has to do with a certain disdain that some psychoanalysts have of the use that some academics make of Lacan and psychoanalysis. I have no sympathy for this position. Lacan's work is out there for people to use as they will, and I believe psychoanalysts must accept that academics who are not psychoanalysts will read and study and use Lacan's work in their own way. Indeed, as I have argued elsewhere, the acceptance of Lacan in the academic community was crucial for establishing some place for his work in the United States when the clinical community rejected it entirely.[8] Beyond that particular issue among psychoanalysts, I will also note a general disdain, to use the word again, for the university and university discourse so common generally in the United States, to a certain extent even among academics. I do not share in that perspective, either. I do not believe that Lacan developed his theory of the four discourses in order to assert any moral superiority of one over another, but rather only to highlight how the different components of a discourse can relate to one another in different configurations and to different results.

I would like to shift gears and approach this distinction between other uses of psychoanalysis and the one that I am proposing here from a

[8] See Thomas Svolos, "Jacques Lacan, Reader," Chapter 2 in *Twenty-First Century Psychoanalysis*, London, Karnac, 2017, pages 13–23, for a discussion of the reception of Lacan in the United States.

different vantage point: through a reading of the ways in which Lacan deployed the concepts of knowledge and truth in his work.

In the 1930s through say the 1950s, for Lacan, truth is the ultimate horizon of the analytic experience.[9] This is developed in a number of different ways. It could be the truth of the encounter with death, or the truth of full speech but, in any case, this truth is to be found as something hidden, which the analyst is seeking.[10] Lacan takes this notion from Heidegger's concept of truth and uses it in his early formulations of the unconscious.[11] This hidden truth, that will evolve with time to become the symbolic truth, is hidden beneath the imaginary, and one of the forms of the imaginary he develops is that of knowledge. Knowledge is always distinct from truth for Lacan, and a key formulation in his early work is that knowledge is fundamentally paranoiac, and this knowledge is linked to the ego and thought, dimensions of the imaginary.[12] Truth, on the other hand, is linked to the symbolic and the treasure trove of signifiers, and it represents the aim of the analytic experience in the early Lacan. In the early Lacan, the analytic process is to cut through the imaginary (in the context of this discussion, the knowledge) in order to reach the truth found at the symbolic.

By the end of his work, Lacan's position on this has shifted. Truth no longer has the privileged position, but itself can have the qualities of a

[9] For a greater elaboration of this trajectory, see chapter 1, "False Aims, Partial Aims," in Thomas Svolos, *The Aims of Analysis: Miami Seminar on the Late Lacan*, *ibid.*

[10] For example, in his seminal paper from 1953 "The Function and Field of Speech and Language in Psychoanalysis", Lacan noted that "The unconscious is the chapter of my history that is marked by a blank or occupied by a lie: it is the censored chapter. But the truth can be refound; most often it has already been written elsewhere." Jacques Lacan, *Écrits: The First Complete Edition in English*, *op. cit.*, page 215. On the encounter with death, see, for example, Lacan's comment that "Here the natural individual is regarded as nil, since the human subject is nothing, in effect, before the absolute Master that death is for him." Jacques Lacan, "Aggressiveness in Psychoanalysis" in *Écrits: The First Complete Edition in English*, *op. cit*, page 98.

[11] A representative comment is "When we are open to hearing the way in which Martin Heidegger uncovers for us in the word *alethes* the play of truth, we merely rediscover a secret to which truth has always initiated her lovers, and through which they have learned that it is in hiding that she offers herself to them most truly." Jacques Lacan, "Seminar on 'The Purloined Letter" in *Écrits: The First Complete Edition in English*, *op. cit*, page 15.

[12] In "The Mirror Stage as Formative of the *I* Function," Lacan noted that "human knowledge is more independent than animal knowledge from the force field of desire because of the social dialectic that structures human knowledge as paranoiac." *Écrits: The First Complete Edition in English*, *op. cit*, page 77.

mirage.[13] The Other no longer exists as a complete and consistent Other (consistency always a property of the imaginary, we might add).[14] The symbolic is no longer the ultimate horizon of the psyche. An equally significant transformation is Lacan's notion of knowledge in his final work, one in which knowledge is tied to modern science and is represented by letters.[15] Knowledge is no longer aligned with the imaginary as much as with the real, and the logic of the real, all based on the distinction Lacan articulates between premodern and modern thought.[16] Lacan adopts this from his reading of modern science, and this is aligned with all of Jacques-Alain Miller's work developing the formulation of the real unconscious, as that which is beneath the symbolic or transferential unconscious.[17]

It is interesting to note that this shift of knowledge from the imaginary to the real also corresponds with a shift in the place of jouissance. As Miller develops very carefully in his paper on "The Six Paradigms of Jouissance," jouissance is originally conceived as existing in the imaginary, but by the final phase of Lacan's work is distinctly aligned with the real.[18]

It needs to be noted that this knowledge in the real is singular for each subject and does not represent any form of generalized knowledge. Indeed, playing on the distinction in French between the two words for knowledge—savoir and connaissance—Lacan develops in "Radiophonie"

---

[13] Lacan speaks of the "mirage of truth" in "The Freudian Thing," *Écrits: The First Complete Edition in English, op. cit*, page 340.

[14] A key instance of this is Lacan's use, in "The Subversion of the Subject and the Dialectic of Desire," of the concept of the lack in the Other: "signifier of a lack in the Other, a lack inherent in the Other's very function as the treasure trove of signifiers." *Écrits: The First Complete Edition in English, op. cit.*, page 693.

[15] This development of the letter as linked to logic and the real and knowledge is articulated through many chapters of Jacques Lacan, *The Seminar of Jacques Lacan: Book XX: Encore (1972–1973)*, New York, W. W. Norton, 1998.

[16] See Jacques Lacan, *The Seminar of Jacques Lacan: Book XX: Encore (1972–1973), op. cit.*, page 128. For a more extensive development of this, see Chapter 14, "*Encore*, encore: knowledge" in Thomas Svolos, *Twenty-first Century Psychoanalysis, op. cit.*, pages 159–169.

[17] See, for example, Jacques-Alain Miller, "The Real Unconscious," *The Lacanian* Review, 6, Fall 2018, pages 29–46.

[18] Jacques-Alain Miller, "Six Paradigms of Jouissance," *Psychoanalytical Notebooks*, 34, December 2019, pages 11–80.

a particular hypothesis about that.[19] My reading of this is that savoir is associated with real knowledge, singular knowledge, knowledge as letter, and knowledge in the real. This is the knowledge at stake that I discussed earlier regarding the Discourse of the Analyst and represents, in many ways, the final aim of the analyst in the analytic experience. Connaissance, on the other hand, becomes a form of imaginarized knowledge, and one that Lacan links in "Radiophonie" to Hegel and the approach to totalizing or dialectical knowledge.

The reason that I bring forth all this esoteric Lacanian theory is to point out the way in which it situates, from within the perspective of psychoanalysis, a type of knowledge that is singular and real, that of savoir, and distinction between that and a form of imaginary knowledge as developed by Lacan. I believe that this distinction is another way of formulating the way in which I would like to separate what I consider a psychoanalytic interpretation in the Discourse of the Analyst (where knowledge is in the form of savoir) from other ways that scholars will use psychoanalysis in interpretation in the Discourse of the University, where knowledge is more in the form of connaissance.

I assert though that this is not a value judgement about which discourse should have precedence or the final word, as we say. I have read and continue to read and study the work of Fredric Jameson and Slavoj Zizek. What I want to do with these opening remarks, rather, was describe from a psychoanalytic perspective something of the particularity of the way in which a psychoanalyst's interpretation might differ from those operating in a different discursive framework.

[19] See especially Lacan's answer to question 6 in Jacques Lacan, "Radiophonie," *Scilicet*, 2/3, Paris, Seuil, 1970, pp. 55–99.

Part II

Identity

I was invited by Lacanian Compass Miami to present a Seminar, which I gave on October 26, 2019, a transcript of which was later published as The Aims of Analysis: Miami Seminar on the Late Lacan. *The night before the seminar, I presented the following talk, which was structured in the form of a conversation, also at the invitation of Lacanian Compass Miami, that was open to the general public. I was asked by Isolda Alvarez Arango, who was the director of the Florida group at that moment, to speak about a topical theme that would be relevant for a general audience that included many students in college and students within the psychoanalytic institute in Miami. In our conversation on possible themes, we settled on identity and groups, as issues associated with them were at the time and remain quite prominent in the political and social debates of our moment. My hypothesis is that identity (at what Lacan describes as the imaginary level) is of greater importance today with a relative weakening of the power of the symbolic order. This leads to more group formation based on identity, which has significant political consequences.*

2

New Forms of Identity and Groups in Postmodernity

Abstract Identity is complex—incorporating dimensions of the imaginary (body image, appearance), the symbolic (role, place in society, values, belief structure), and the real (generally opaque to the person, the libidinal dimension). The relationship of and construction of identity is based, in part, on the ways in which these different dimensions are articulated for any person. Furthermore, that process itself is dependent on historically changing social structures whose impact on the development of identity and subjectivity are both manifest and, at times, difficult to read. This is true for both individual identity and the collective identity that is the functioning of groups. In postmodernity, the symbolic order's dominance over other orders has been replaced with novel forms of identity and groups, not necessarily mediated through the symbolic.

Keywords Identity construction • Group formation • Postmodernity • Imaginary • Symbolic • Real

Isolda Alvarez Arango: Hello. Hi, good evening. Thank you so much for being here with us today. Thank you, Tom, who has been traveling from Omaha, Nebraska, to talk today about new forms of identity and how we form groups in postmodernity. Tom Svolos is a psychoanalyst, a

T. Svolos, *Culture and Politics on the Couch*, The Palgrave Lacan Series,
https://doi.org/10.1007/978-3-031-61365-4_2

psychiatrist, and a member of the New Lacanian School and the World Association of Psychoanalysis. He practices in Omaha, Nebraska, where he serves as Professor of Psychiatry at the Creighton University School of Medicine. He is also the author of the book *Twenty-first Century Psychoanalysis*. Today, we are going to be talking about this thing that we call "Identity."

So, I was talking with Tom about this, and we cannot deny the fact that our psyche, our subjectivity has changed. In fact, for the psychoanalytical field, a human being is understood more as a speaking being or a speaking body. So, in psychoanalysis, the entity that we think that is commanding our thoughts, our behaviors, our choices, is not especially the self as is taken up by psychology, for example. For us, it is more that weird thing that we call the unconscious. Freud proposed this approach, or this practice, and the conception of the human being will never be the same. So, psychoanalysis itself has changed as well. It is not the same psychoanalysis that it used to be when Freud invented this approach. We have changes in society and how we organize to live together or try to live together. Following this path, how do we understand identity? Or, what identifies each one of us? Having in mind that for us, the unconscious is kind of the boss of this matter, not the soul.

So, about this, Tom, before we talk about the new forms of identity or groups in postmodernity, would you please tell us, what is an identity? And, also, tell us if you believe this notion is only to refer to sexuality, because many people sometimes think that when you talk about identity, you are only talking about sexuality. Because we all have certain traits that help us to recognize ourselves, to recognize certain social roles. But, we also have our sexual orientation as well, we have family values, political affiliations, and, for some, religious identities linked to religious beliefs. So, is this identity?

Thomas Svolos: Thank you. I want to first thank Lacanian Compass Miami for the invitation to be here together with many old friends. We have worked together many times over the years here in Miami and elsewhere in the United States, and I am very happy to see friends from elsewhere here as well, some folks that I have had the opportunity to work together with before. So, thank you for the invitation and the hospitality.

Isolda, thank you for this question and let me start, before we talk about the new forms, either of identity or group, by just laying a few coordinates that I think represent ways that people have thought about identity and group that are very old. I think one of them has to do with your identification, your relationship with yourself as a body. And you perceive that primarily, for most people, visually. So, it is an image of your body. For a lot of people, this is what you think of. Well, this is what I am. (pointing at self) I am the thing that exists when I look in a mirror. That is me. That is my identity. It is an identity based on an image of the body and this was one of Lacan's very first . . . I know the audience is quite varied in its familiarity with psychoanalytic terminology, so please interrupt me if I jump too quickly. Jacques Lacan was a French psychoanalyst who followed the work of Sigmund Freud, and many of us here work in the School and the tradition that Lacan founded. So, one of Jacques Lacan's first contributions about this question of identity was the identity that one takes through an image in the mirror.[1] And, this is an old notion of identity, and it is based on looks. When one thinks about how you would form a group based on this identity, the group is people who look like me and people who I don't identify with are the people who look different from me. This way of thinking about it seems very simple, but it is something that still exists today, even though it is very old.

The way that this gets configured in terms of group formation is often the distinction then between the people who look like me and the "other" people. In politics, it is the notion of friends and enemies that has been around for a long time, but it is an idea whose attraction has come and gone over the last couple of hundred years as a way of thinking. There have been, since the time of the Enlightenment, periods where we have had movements where people were interested in getting beyond that. This is the belief in universalism, a universal society, or the belief that we can form international associations that will organize peaceful coexistence of societies across the globe. This was a dream, for example, of Immanuel Kant, who wrote a paper "Towards Perpetual Peace" that

[1] Jacques Lacan, "The Mirror Stage as Formative of the I Function as Revealed in Psychoanalytic Experience," in *Écrits: The First Complete Edition in English*, *op. cit.*, pages. 75–81.

proposed this.[2] Many people hoped that we could resolve conflicts through associations of people coming together. But, as we see in politics and certainly, we see in this country today and across the globe today, the notion of friend and enemy as an organizer of political groups has not disappeared at all. And, in fact, the politics and the dynamics of group formation that organizes around this at a societal and political level in some ways replicates how a similar phenomenon plays out at a familial level in love, hate, and rivalry—the relations that occur between siblings within families, the tensions and the emotions that occur among them. Anyhow, some groups form on the basis of this logic. Sometimes, those groups are formed through love, a positive identification with people who look like me. But, we must not neglect how hate can be a formative factor, through what I call negative identification. "I don't want to be like that person over there, so I am going to create a group based on people who are not that." And, this operates at a political level as well. This was part of the functioning of Trump's candidacy and presidency and the way he constructed his voting public, which is, "We don't want to be like those, the un-American people, over there." But it is also true on the left as well. If you look at the candidacy of Bernie Sanders, it is very interesting. "We do not want to be like those 1 percenters." Even though there were some 1 percenters who supported the Bernie Sanders' candidacy, the campaign was built around the negative identification with the people who live in the 1%: "I don't want to be like that."[3] This identity based on positive image or negative image is a very old notion of identity, but, for Lacan at least, it is not the final word. It is not the truth to who I am as a person. And then, the psychoanalytic message here, we could even say, is one that beneath your imaginary identity, the one that you are aware of and consciously adopt, there is something else and Freud, the psychoanalyst Sigmund Freud, referred to that as the unconscious.

Alvarez Arango: So, Tom, based on this, we can say that we are no longer within universalism's regime? This was a regime preached and established by Christianity, for example. This idea that we were able to find the

[2] Immanuel Kant, *"Towards Perpetual Peace" and Other Writings on Politics, Peace, and History*, New Haven, Yale University Press, 2006.

[3] See Chap. 6 in this book for a more extensive development of this point.

universal truth, "a" universal truth, right? Aristotle proposed the same thing before Christianity, but right now, it is another order. There is something different that is organizing our experience of identity. But nowadays, the notion of relativity that was introduced by postmodernism is all over the place. There has been a change in the core of our identity, and these fads surrounding relativity have affected the way or changed the way in which we form groups today.

Svolos: The reference to Christianity is important and let's start maybe by going back to that. Because, for the most part, prior to the advent of Judaism and the Judeo-Christian tradition, there were many gods. And, if you look at the pre-Christian societies in the ancient world, people existed in a society and they had their, in many cases, gods, many gods, and if you took over another society, you took over their gods as well. It was a polytheistic world. And the people adapted to that world. And there was obviously conflict mediated that way. With Christianity, in particular, you get the introduction of a single God and the definition of a single truth that applies to everyone. I think an important fact of the Christian tradition is the introduction of the importance of language in mediating that truth through the Word of God. This introduces universalism and a universal rule of law, the Word of God. This has an effect, I think, on how people construct their identity in a way that is different from the pre-Christian era. You can read, for example, a writer like Erich Auerbach, who wrote a lot about literature and his analysis of the change that occurs from Homer, for example, and the subjectivity that existed for an ancient Greek in the pre-Christian era and how that is different from what you find in the Christian era.[4] What are the issues that pertain there to identity? One is that there is a single truth, there is a single God, and that everyone lives in that world. It is a God for everyone, it is a universal God. What St. Paul contributed to the church was the fact that anybody could be a member of the church.[5] Prior to this moment, gods were tied to particular groups. There were different gods, and there was a toleration of the fact that this person believes in this god in this social

---

[4] Erich Auerbach, *Mimesis: The Representation of Reality in Western Literature*, Princeton, Princeton University Press, 1953.

[5] For a more extended discussion of this, see chapter 8, "The Body Politic," in Thomas Svolos, *Twenty-first Century Psychoanalysis*, *op. cit.*, pages 93–102.

group and that person believes in that god in another social group. Now, there is one God, but anybody can become part of that group simply by going through the rituals it takes to become a Christian. And the impact of this is significant in several ways regarding identity. First, this is the moment of an introduction of a universalism, for all, and the second is that your identity is, in a sense, then less tied up with your image and more tied up with your words. Think of, for example, how we construct marriage now in the Judeo-Christian world. It is based on a symbolic vow. It is based on the words you speak from one person to another that makes it happen. You might say that is a positive sign of the identity, the way your identity is linked to your speech, but there is also this flip side to it, which is in your commitment to this principle, say, you have to sacrifice certain things about yourself to become a member of that church, a certain submission. In Luke, Jesus says something, which I will paraphrase, "If you wish to be one of my disciples, you have to sever your ties with your family, with your spouse and so forth and so on."[6] In taking on the cause, say, of Christianity, you have to sever those connections that meant something to you. In this form of identity, there is a necessity of a sacrifice for something. This is not only true from the religious perspective. Take Kant, for example, if you study modern philosophy and examine what Kant had to say in the *Critique of Practical Reason,* you find an interesting definition of what constitutes the moral action. The moral thing to do cannot be something that you are choosing for a pathological reason, where "pathology" is defined as something that serves your personal interest, because it makes you feel good, but, rather, it has to be something that fulfills a law that would apply universally. So, there is a sacrificial character that is tied up in this kind of identity, and you see it in an extreme form in the Christian tradition of self-flagellation, the pain that must come from taking on an identity like this. And, this is no less prevalent today. A book was recently published by Tom Holland called, I believe, *Dominion*, in which he traces the impact of this kind of thought of Christianity and universalism into modern secular thought of the Enlightenment.[7] So, it still has a power.

---

[6] Luke 14:26.

[7] Tom Holland, *Dominion: The Making of the Western World*, London, Little, Brown, 2009.

Now, let me say that one of Jacques Lacan's first ways of putting the two forms of identity into relationship was to say that when you look beyond the imaginary identities that people have, how they see themselves, you find a symbolic identity in their unconscious, formed on the basis of phenomena related to how they were raised, the facts of the parents, the place that was made for them within the family, the symbolic universe that the parents created for the child, and so forth. So, for Lacan, these two different ways of forming identity are related in ways that have relevance in the practice of psychoanalysis.

Alvarez Arango: So, we first have the imaginary, which was what you said before, based on the image. Someone looks like me, or someone doesn't look like me, so I feel that I might belong with or not belong with that person. And, then, the symbolic moment, let's say. Are we still in that moment today? In the symbolism that helps us to organize, to identify based on what you were saying related to universal structures—does that symbolic form of identity still exist today?

Svolos: I think we are in a different place. It does not mean that these other structures of identity aren't operative, but I think what has happened in our world today is that these symbolic structures like the church, which provided meaning and identity and so forth, have weakened substantially. What have we seen that has come out of that shift? Take, for example, the issues of gender and sexuality. One of the things that defined Lacan's perspective on sexuality is that sexuality is something problematic for all of us, every speaking being must negotiate relationships and intimacy, and generally do that using language. And, language itself is inherently problematic. There are inherent failures of communication related to language—often our intended message is not heard the way we want by the people we talk with. Animals can have, we imagine, animal sexuality in a non-problematic way. A dog seems to have no problem having sexual interaction with other dogs, human beings, pieces of furniture, and so forth, and obtaining pleasure in a way that doesn't seem to cause any distress or anything.

Alvarez Arango: At least we don't know that any dog is asking its partner dog, "What do you mean?"

Svolos: Exactly.

Alvarez Arango: "What does this mean to you? I mean, did you like it?" No. That doesn't happen.

(laughter)

Svolos: No. But for the human being, we have to negotiate all this with language, which does not allow us to put things into words; or, it does not allow us to put everything we want into words; or, we put things into words, and we accidentally put more than we wanted in the words that we put and have to deal with that. So, it is a problem.

Audience: So, I was going to say, doesn't that tie to our consciousness? Like a dog doesn't have that consciousness inside his brain, well, that we know of. Unlike these creatures, we have evolved to another, *Homo sapiens*.

Svolos: I am not sure about the consciousness of dogs. I think the distinguishing thing is language. The other animals may have some kinds of symbolic ways of communicating, people talk about the bees and social insects like ants and so forth, but not with language. And, language introduces a fundamental problem with regard to sexuality. And, it wasn't just Lacan who observed this. There is an interesting passage in the works of St. Augustine, where he talks about *discordiosum malum*, a fundamental discord in the human as a function of sexuality and society.[8] He did not focus on language as much, but it is much like this notion of Lacan's of the *non-rapport sexual*, or sexual non-relation.

Now, the reason I bring this up is because what the symbolic identities gave us in the Christian tradition were very structured solutions to the problems of sexuality. In the Christian tradition, which I know the most about, there are clear definitions and imperatives for men and women. God created man and woman. This includes all the various passages in the Bible about the creation of men and women and how the affairs between men and women are regulated through what becomes the sacraments of the church and so forth. It is a way of managing, you could say, issues of gender and sexuality that is universal, for everyone. So, if you are a believer in the church, these are the answers. There are men and there

---

[8] For a greater elaboration of this point and issues associated with imaginary, symbolic, and real identity in general, see Thomas Svolos, "The Body Politic" in *Twenty-first Century Psychoanalysis*, *op. cit.*

are women, this is how they relate, and this how we define a marriage. What is a marriage? The church has a very clear answer: This is what a marriage is. So, with what I think we have seen now, and this is the point I want to make about something else, is as those structures have weakened, now we see, "Well, maybe there are many more genders or even some who are beyond gender." There are different ways of thinking about what it is to be a man or to be a woman or a person, or what it is in terms of what one is interested in or attracted to in terms of gender, and sexual practices aren't limited only by what the Church has to say. I just happened to hear last week—I don't know if people follow the Supreme Court—but there was a Supreme Court case around Title IX discrimination and sexual orientation. It was interesting. The Supreme Court justices and the lawyers presenting the case before them were having an intense argument about the difference between gender identity versus sexual orientation and how this applies to Title IX and the rules against discrimination. This type of debate would have been unthinkable fifty years ago—that this would be argued in the Supreme Court. This is a certain sign, to me, of a weakening of the place of the Church's symbolic authority over issues of gender and sexuality.

What is interesting about this is that these ways of configuring gender identity or sexuality were different in the pre-Christian era. As you may know, Michel Foucault was a very prominent French historian. Foucault wrote some books about the ancient Greeks and the Romans, and he identified the ways in which gender and sexual identity or orientation were not as fixed as they came to be in the Christian era.[9] And, for Foucault, who was very involved in gay rights movements in France, this was very important. So, he went back to the pre-Christian era, and he found in his research ways of approaching identity and sexuality that could be used as ways of advocating for rights for gays in France in the 1970s. This was one of his political projects. But, it says something that I think is very important, which is that prior to the advent of Christianity,

[9] Michel Foucault, *The Use of Pleasure: Volume 2 of the History of Sexuality*, New York, Vintage Books, 1990. Michel Foucault, *The Care of the Self: Volume 3 of the History of Sexuality*, New York, Vintage Books, 1988.

there was not a universal structure to the symbolic that led to strict, determined identities.

So, what we are seeing now is that the symbolic is weakened and because of this, we are finding different ways of thinking about oneself as gendered. This has led to new ways of constructing identity. This would be one way to understand the whole issue of transgender or post-binary forms of identity. And, I would argue that, to use the language of domains of imaginary, symbolic and real that Lacan adhered to, we might hypothesize this as a form of an imaginarized real. It is an identity based on the real.

Alvarez Arango: Okay, Tom, based on this, we could say that gender is different than sexuality, right? At least for Lacanian psychoanalysis. So, we say that sexuality goes beyond gender and could be more related to a matter of choice, for example. What did you mean when you said, in some papers that you sent me previous to this conversation, that nowadays sexuality is organized individually by people themselves, one by one, that they choose an identity and orientation? I am guessing that it has to do with this decline that you have discussed about symbolic institutions, which used to provide structure. This has changed now with postmodernity. What more could you say about this?

Svolos: Well, I think, one aspect of it is that there is, in my mind, a very strong distinction between identity in the sense of gender identity, whether it is a traditional male/female or a much more elaborate panoply of identities, and what we Lacanian psychoanalysts call desire, that which brings us excitement or attraction and so forth, what is not without a relationship with sexual orientation or object choice. I think they are very different things. But, one of the social phenomena that I see sometimes regarding how people form groups is a new form of groups, which are groups that develop around those identities. In building a life around that identity linked with such a group, I find that sometimes what may be lost is the fact of desire, of something beyond my identity that defines what I want in the world, something more than just my identity based on this one identity construct.

Alvarez Arango: Okay, so we have this thing that you just touched on. We have many identities or labels within the LGBTQ+ community. We don't deny at all that certain labels help us precisely to make a point about desire or desire of each one, but we can also say that we will have more classifications and more segregation as well because of that. So, what solution do you think would be possible, not like "the solution is . . ." . . . no, not like that, but what do you think about this? If I understand, one of the questions that gets posed in psychoanalysis is who is the person behind the identity? Identity doesn't say everything about someone. Based on that, what does Lacanian psychoanalysis say about this?

Svolos: With the decline of symbolic frameworks of one sort or another, of the universalism and rule of law that comes with a certain form of the symbolic, I think one of the concerns that Lacan raised was about this risk of segregation, a segregation based on identity. And, I would say that we can observe that precise shift to segregation, for example, within the realm of politics and the realm of sexuality. I think what we see today in society is a tendency towards segregation. People end up following and communicating with the people with whom they think alike. In other words, you are grouped: the pro-Trumpers are with the pro-Trumpers, the anti-Trumpers with the anti-Trumpers. There is a tendency in politics for people to segregate into the groups with people they identify with. And, I would contrast that with something you were talking about earlier today, when the two of us were chatting about our agenda. You were telling me about a movie, a documentary movie about a Muslim woman of color who interviewed white supremacists.

Alvarez Arango: *Meeting with the Enemy.*

Svolos: *Meeting with the Enemy.* As you described it, what was interesting about this is that this Muslim woman would interview these white supremacists and, after a while, they would grow to decide that they could form a bond with her, that they had some appreciation of her, and they were able to communicate with her and transcend the segregation that they had formed in their image of her as a Muslim woman of color, even though they identified as white supremacists. Am I right?

Alvarez Arango: Yes, you are right.

Svolos: So, I think in the realm of politics, I believe segregation is a threat to us now, because it tends to bring out hatred and a tendency towards destruction that we can see as the result of that kind of hatred. It feeds the death drive, as Freud described it. I don't know exactly what Lacan had in mind when he talked about the risk of segregation, but when I think of it now, I think it comes with the loss of a belief in a universal or a space of discourse or even just the basic rule of law or an appreciation of difference.[10] It is not all about identity, but a difference and an appreciation for that which is different. Recall that for Lacan, the symbolic was one of the great forms taken by what he called the Other. One of the characteristics of the other is that it is different, it is other than the subject.

Alvarez Arango: Diversity.

Svolos: Yes, you could even say diversity. Jacques-Alain Miller, who is another analyst, once said that Freud's view on love can be organized in two ways: "People have a tendency to fall in love in two different ways. You fall in love with the person who looks like you, who thinks like you, who is a mirror image of you; or you fall in love with your mother."[11]

(Laughter)

Svolos: Yes, it is funny, but note that rather than loving oneself, in loving one's mother, in a sense, one introduces something of difference. I think now we are caught up in a time where people are friends with the people who look like them, but it is no longer only on the basis of looks, it may be the people who share some identity trait, whether it is political or even sexual, and that there is a risk that the appreciation of difference is lost. Does that make sense?

Alvarez Arango: Yes. Well, to me. Does that make sense for you in the audience? Maybe? A little bit. Okay. So, the idea for this event today is to conduct this more like a conversation, not a lecture. So, it is open for you to make questions or comments. I have some questions that some of my students sent me. Do you want me to go over these questions?

Svolos: Pick ones that maybe we haven't already talked about. Some of these we may have already discussed.

Alvarez Arango: Okay, here is one interesting. Do we need identity?

Svolos: Do we need identity?

---

[10] Lacan wrote, for example, that "Our future as common markets will be balanced by an increasingly hard-line extension of the process of segregation." Jacques Lacan, "Proposition of 9 October 1967 on the Psychoanalyst of the School," accessed on November 19, 2022, at https://lacancircle.com.au/wpcontent/uploads/2017/11/Proposition_of_9_October.pdf.

[11] Jacques-Alain Miller, "We Love the One Who Responds to Our Question: 'Who Am I?'" *Psychologies Magazine*, Issue 278, October 2008.

Alvarez Arango: Yes. Can we be around without any identity?

Audience: Animals don't have identities. They just go about not putting a label to them.

Svolos: Let's start and just talk about simple imaginary identification. We are going to have some image of who we are. Most every person, at least. The issue is, what weight do you give to it? I mean, how does it figure in your life? What do you do with it? To me, it would be difficult to conceive of not having an identity. What is interesting is what you do with it, more than it being inherently bad. To not have an ego, an identity, is difficult for most to conceive. It would be a dream. You could almost say that it would be a kind of Kantian dream, which then turns into a nightmare. In a sense, Lacan's point about Kant is Kant leads to Sade, because if everything that I might have or think about as my personal interest is pathological or bad as Kant suggested, I have to do everything for a universal cause outside of me. In a way, what Kant called pathological interest is aligned in a sense with the ego.[12] And, Kantian ethics calls for an effort to make the ego and our personal and pathological interests go away completely, but I don't think that is such a good answer, because I think you end up with self-destruction without an identity. That would be my preliminary answer to the question about if you can do without an identity. It leads to self destruction.

Alvarez Arango: I there is anyone in the audience with a question?

Audience: The thing about identity I was going to say is that many times people have identities, but sometimes they don't address them. That is the thing. You might have them in the back of your head, you know, some of us, most of us in Miami, have identities also from the places that we are from, and they are in the back of our heads, but we don't really sit down and write down, you know, "I am this and I am that." I guess it depends how much you decide to address and label yourself as something.

Svolos: And I would say in response that another lesson of psychoanalysis is that people will come in to see an analyst thinking they are one thing and then find out, hmmm, maybe that wasn't exactly the case. I

---

[12] See Jacques Lacan, "Kant with Sade," *Écrits: The First Complete Edition in English*, *op. cit.*, pp. 645–70.

remember a session with somebody, who was talking about a book that was very important for this person, always thinking that she was one character in the book with whom she strongly identified, but then something happened in her analysis—I think it was a slip of the tongue—and the patient all of a sudden said, "Oh my gosh, all along I thought I was this person, but, in reality, I think I am really this other character in the book." So, identities are fluid. They can be fluid. And, we can make mistakes about them. As you know, we have this phrase in English, "mistaken identity." We are often mistaken about our identities. That is another part of the first thing Lacan had to say about identities, namely that you can say every identity is a mistaken identity to some degree, but to not have any identity at all might be the biggest mistake, to think you can do without it.

Audience: How can you have a mistaken identity if the past is the past and the present is constantly changing? You are constantly creating yourself as a new individual. There are different components that make up you as a person, so I don't think there is a set identity, because you are always constantly changing. You, for example, are not just a psychoanalyst, you are not just a speaker. It is more than that. I just feel that the present, the future, and the past, it all has to do with who you are, and it defines you, because obviously you can't go back to the past, but you will always be . . . like a scar. You have a scar; it will always stay on your body for the rest of your life. So, all of these components make up who you are, so I don't think it is like a set identity because you are always evolving. It is not really a question; it was just a comment.

Svolos: Yes, it is a comment, and I will respond to it this way. I think one of the ways of thinking about what the unconscious is, it may not be the best, but I think it is of some use, is the fact that in a way, depending on how you settled your affairs with the past, the past may not be the past. The past may be your present. You gave an example of a scar, which is a good example because it signals a trauma, something bad happened and you got an injury, and you got a wound.

Audience: But, you won't always symbolize it as a negative.

Svolos: Well, correct. But, words cause wounds. Words cause scars. Much of what people talk about in analysis is the words that have affected them in their lives, affected them in their experiences of their body that go back to when they were very young. And those words have an impact on the body and sometimes, the impact of those words on the body is not known to the person when it happened consciously. It is not in your awareness, but it affects your life, throughout your life, in the way that the unconscious can have an impact without you being aware of it. And, let me add, that I believe that these scars, these wounds, these words function in a way that is very different from the avowed identities and labels that we have been speaking about.

So, it is not a great metaphor, but let me offer this metaphor: your image of yourself is your screen on the computer, but there is a hard drive that has all kinds of stuff in it that makes things pop up on the screen and you don't know why, "Why is that popping up on the screen now?" One of the things you can experience in a psychoanalysis, going through a psychoanalysis, which the analysts in the room have all done, is to come to terms with these things that were in the past but continued to have a life in your present. And, then, maybe after confronting them, the past doesn't have the same effect. It is always something that was in your past, but with the experience of psychoanalysis, you can then leave it in your past, and it is no longer part of your present. This is another way to describe something that is part of the psychoanalytic experience. That would be my response to your comment.

Audience: Now that we are on the topic of the unconscious, is there ever a way to control the unconscious? And if there is, what is that line between the unconscious and the conscious? Does that make sense?

Svolos: It does. It is an interesting question. I don't think we can control the unconscious. You could almost say that something that is part of the unconscious is something you couldn't control at the moment it happened, and so it ends up in the unconscious. One of Freud's hypotheses about this came from his experience in working with war veterans who had seen bad things in World War I and also people who had accidents with the railroads, which affected a lot of people back then—rail workers would have serious accidents.[13] Freud's hypothesis was that the trauma

[13] Sigmund Freud, "Beyond the Pleasure Principle," *The Standard Edition of the Complete Psychological Works of Sigmund Freud*, Vol. 18, London, Hogarth, 1955, pages 7–64. See also a greater elaboration of this in Thomas Svolos, "Terrible Events and Their Relation to the Universal Trauma of Subjectivity," *Twenty-First Century Psychoanalysis, Op. cit.*, pages 37–56.

results from the fact that something overwhelms your ability to have a controlled, measured response to it. Your mind, let's say, is overwhelmed by something horrible, such as death, that you witnessed, or something like that. And, so, what happens is the thing that you witnessed ends up in your unconscious, along with all of the affect that came with it. All of the anguish and the anxiety and so forth just starts floating around and affecting your life in all kinds of different ways. So, Freud's thought really was that when you can't control your response to something, it ends up as unconscious. And, you might say that in a way, you could understand the process of working through something traumatic through psychoanalysis as taking hold of that bad thing that happened and managing with it in a different way so that you have a little bit more control over it. So, you can't control the unconscious, but a part of psychoanalysis might be to bring something back into consciousness so that you can have a controlled response to it, in such a way that you can deal with it that gives you room to maneuver that maybe you didn't have before.

Audience: First, I want to say something in reference to homosexuality: how Freud was the first to take homosexuality out of the category of perversion, and that was in 1901. I always say jokingly, but seriously jokingly, that the gay community owes a statue to Freud, because he was the first one in the Victorian era to say something like that. He took a risk, and it had some effect on his life. So, talking again about the changes of the symbolic, I love the way that you put it, because you put it in terms of history. So, we called it the decline of the monopoly of the symbolic, but it is not really a decline, it is a change, it is a preliminary change and that is very important to note because a new way, a new status of the symbolic emerges that is more plural, more liquid. The new regime has good things and bad things, as did the old regime. The new regime includes new forms of sexuality as new forms of identity, and the old regime did not include those forms before, which were rejected. But one delusion that you pointed out and maybe you could say more about it, is the delusion that these changes will solve the problem of identity. Because the real problem for psychoanalysis is there is always a dissonance, a disagreement between jouissance, the enjoyment of the body, and the meaning that we give to that body and that scar. So, we have identities that are related to the image, makeup/no makeup, identities that are more related to the symbolic, Christian/not Christian, boy/girl. But, we also have these scars and the meaning that we gave to these scars. I am thinking about how to exemplify that. Someone told me that he was surprised, because talking with his brothers, he discovered that they think he was the preferred one among his siblings, but he always had this fantasy that the mother treated him very specially because he was *pobrecito*, poor guy. So, the thing was there, it was fixed, it was something that the mother put in his brothers, he was the most dedicated, the most taken care of, the preferred one, but he doesn't read it that way. And the dimension of the meaning is very important because something emerged that is always in a fight with this identity. There is always dissonance, so maybe you could say something more about the relationship between identity, body, and meaning that is special.

Svolos: Thank you. Let me say first going back to your initial comment about Freud: it is Freud who, in 1905, I think it was, talked about the essential bisexuality of everybody.[14] In other words, his theory about sexuality was that it ends up eventually for most getting—he uses funny metaphors—into certain tracks, but at a certain level, everybody is essentially bisexual, there is an indeterminate quality to it. So, not only was Freud important for the point you made regarding homosexuality, but he was the first one to even speak of inherent bisexuality, or one might even say nonbinary quality to the polymorphous perversity of the speaking being, to use one phrase of his.

About this other point, yes, I think what you said is important, which is that one of the struggles we deal with is the fact that you could say for every speaking being, the image we have of our self, the meaning we give to our life, and the way we experience our body are not aligned—there is conflict and discord. Only in what we call fantasy do we find the idea of coherence and achieving balance and unity and these kinds of things, which is something that people strive for and talk about. I find that the people come to see me often with complaints about how they are failing to find balance and coherence. I hear demands, such as "Give me work/life balance" or statements such as "My wife and I need to find a

[14] Sigmund Freud, "Three Essays on the Theory of Sexuality," *The Standard Edition of the Complete Psychological Works of Sigmund Freud*, Vol. 7, London, Hogarth, 1955, pages 125–248.

harmonious relationship." Demands like that are often part of the reason to seek an analyst, but what ends up transpiring as people work is they recognize there is an imbalance and a tension and that their initial demand is impossible, but at the same time that they find ways to manage with the discord, to live with it. It is interesting to me that you bring this up, because when Lacan talks about all premodern forms of philosophy and knowledge and science, he states that they are based on a fantasy of the inscription of the sexual link. Everything about premodern thought, for Lacan, included a belief in this kind of harmony. For example, in Aristotle, there is a notion of the harmony between the individual and society—individuals can have harmonious relationships with society. I don't think so. No, I don't. And I don't mean to be pessimistic, but I think there are times where you make your peace with society, but there are times where you are in conflict. And, believing that the solution is to achieve harmony is impossible. The solution is to manage the conflict, to know how to deal with the conflict. And the conflict can be interesting, too. I mean: you can have fun with it and so forth. So, it is not all a bad thing. I think this question is a good one because it speaks to a kind of tension that is part of being human, and I think a part of it for us, and this goes back to the point I made earlier, is a function of language, because language, which is how we engage with others, is not a perfect communication system. I intend to say something. No matter how carefully I try to say it, what I say will be heard differently by the person I say it to. You can't speak in such a way to perfectly transmit your intent. There isn't perfect communication where I can put my thought into words, and the words will be heard the way I want them to be heard. It leaves us with a problem in how we negotiate with ourselves and with others that can't be transcended.

Audience: You mentioned new forms of identities and groups formed in postmodern times and now in our times. But at the same time, technology has changed, and the internet has come into play. Did that change or affect anything in terms of how these groups were forming? You mentioned how an aspect of forming group identity was based off how we look, and now on the internet, you are not even seeing the person anymore. You are not making a relationship anymore with the body of someone doing something out in the world. It is more just sending messages to each other. How has this changed group formation?

Svolos: I will answer your question in this way. Hyde Park in London, 100 years ago, was a social gathering place. it was like a nondigital internet, where people would go to communicate with one another and offer their opinions on one thing or another. People would get up and start talking. To get themselves heard more, they would stand on top of things like boxes and crates, and it is where the phrase "to get up on a soapbox" comes from, because people would take these shipping crates, and they would stand on them and talk about whatever political or social matter they wanted to talk about. I think the internet is a giant soapbox. You can go on the internet on Facebook, Twitter, Instagram, or whatever media form and say what you want, post pictures. I would say the image is not absent from social media or the internet, because you can fashion your image. You can create avatars, your image, "This is going to be my image on Twitter." Lacanian Compass has a Twitter page, which I actually run, and I know we have the Lacanian Compass symbol as the little symbol for the Lacanian Compass Twitter page. I don't know about Facebook and all the other kinds of social media, but I understand in many of them, you can pick the image you want for yourself, and that image is a part of it. With Snapchat and Instagram, I know the images, little videos or images, are a part of the communication.

In fact, I would even say that in postmodernity, the image is more important than it was before. Guy Debord drew our attention to this in the 1960s, in a book called *The Society of the Spectacle*, the key text associated with the Situationist movement, which was a French movement from the 1960s.[15] One of the things he was focused on was a return of the importance of the image in society and that had to do with the development of television, obviously movies and then television, and now the internet. So, I almost think we have not seen a decline in the image at all; if anything, the image is more ascendant. It is stronger than ever.

Let me just say one additional thing about group formation, because there is one other thing I would want to say about groups that speaks to a different way of forming groups. Lacan went to England after World

[15] Guy Debord, *The Society of the Spectacle*, New York, Zone Books, 1994.

War II, in 1946, to study how the English psychiatrists managed the war effort compared to the French. It was not a high point for the French, World War II: I hope you recognize that the French got rolled over by the Germans, and there were concerns about the ways in which some French collaborated with the German occupiers by turning in Jews to the Gestapo, and it was an embarrassing moment for the French. So, I believe that a group of French psychiatrists, interested in how the British managed psychiatry in the war, sent Lacan, who was a psychiatrist, to study the English. And, he got interested in the work of some English analysts such as Bion and Rickman and how they dealt with delinquent soldiers, soldiers who lost heart, who couldn't fight, who had to be removed from fighting units, and how could they help them recover their morale.[16] So, what the British did was not to punish them, but house them in a kind of hospital where they put them in groups and gave them tasks. The soldiers had to figure out how to deal with it, whatever the job was. "You are responsible for cooking," "You are responsible for this," "You are responsible for that." And, Lacan studied this and how they did it. There was one feature of this that I think is very important, which is the way that the groups were organized: the people had to bond together and find ways of creating a bond without the presence of a leader. The groups functioned without a leader, not based on a universal principle. Another analyst, Éric Laurent, reading this, emphasized the dimension of horizontal identification that is not oriented around a universal, which I know is a technical way of putting it.[17] But the idea is, you would take people who were different from one another, and with the guidance of the institution they would form a group, not because they all are aligned with some universal belief or leader, but because they have a task to complete, something to do and that forms the group. So, this is a different kind of way of thinking about group formation. A group can form that includes people who are very different, but because of a shared task that they are focused on, they will come together as a group and do it without a leader or universal belief, such as a church or army hierarchy. I will give

[16] You may read Lacan's description of this in Jacques Lacan, "British Psychiatry and the War," *Psychoanalytic Notebooks*, #33 [*The Real and the Social Bond*], June 2019, pages 11–58.

[17] Éric Laurent, "The Real and the Group," *Psychoanalytic Notebooks*, #33, [*The Real and the Social Bond*], June 2019, pages 59–86.

you a bizarre example, maybe, but it is interesting. I think one of the key cultural documents through which to study groups these days is the television series "The Wire," which I am a big fan of. We already talked about it a little earlier today. It is fictional, but very close to a documentary, as the creator was a journalist for many years in Baltimore. It is very much based on the reality of the reporting of the creators. The show depicts the gang life of drug dealers in Baltimore, their interactions with the police, but also, over the five years of the show, includes the school system, politics, and the newspapers in the city. So, there are several different ways you can look at groupings in "The Wire." One is traditional groups, such as families. People are born into a family of drug dealers, they continue to deal drugs, and so forth. And this is a very simplistic view. Very different from that would be people who get together, I am thinking now of the police officers, some of them, who get together with their fellow police officers based on the fact that they like to beat people up, a form of aggressive libido. So, there is a group of police officers in this series who you can see bond with the other officers because of what they refer to as the "Western District Way." This phrase aligns with a district of the city and the way some of the police act, in groups. Because in the Western District, the police beat people up on the street and lock them up. They get shared pleasure out of enacting their aggression on criminals. They are not particularly effective police officers; they just run around and beat up criminals and lock them up, and they think that is policing. But, it is also a kind of identity and group formation based on an enjoyment that they experience, being aggressive. I was talking about this earlier, namely an identification they get, not because they want to uphold the law, but just because they enjoy being aggressive—which I define as a real versus symbolic identification. But there are these other interesting groupings that happen in this series. I am thinking in particular of several officers who develop these interesting group relationships, in one case with a guy who is a heroin addict—"Bubs"—for people who have seen the series. He is an informant, and they know he is a heroin addict. They give him money, and he gives them information about drug dealers. They give him money knowing that he is going to take the money and go and buy heroin with it. They don't arrest him, but they form a bond because he helps them, and they help him deal with some particularly unsavory characters in the drug dealing world. Or, there is another character, who is quite interesting: Omar. Omar is a guy who robs drug dealers and shoots them and kills them. He is a murderer, and he steals from the drug dealers. He was President Obama's favorite character. There is an interview, which is quite remarkable. When he was president, Barack Obama interviewed David Simon, the creator of "The Wire," in the White House, in a recorded video where the president was the interviewer.[18] This is the President of the United States interviewing, not being interviewed. It is very fun to watch. Anyhow, Obama loved Omar, and Omar is a guy who was a criminal who robbed drug dealers. But there is a moment in the movie where Omar forms a relationship with the police. The police know he is a murderer, but they come together for a common cause. So, this is a case where there is absolute difference. Right? On the one hand, you have the police; on the other hand, you have someone who is a known murderer, and, in spite of the difference, there is a transcending of the difference through coming together as group for a shared task, which is to take down one of the gang leaders. Such groups are not based on a universal standard that group members have to believe in, sign up for, such as sacrificing for the higher cause. It is a transient group. It gets to the issue alluded to earlier, the idea that things are not so stable now. Well, you can form these unstable, *ad hoc* groups that are very interesting. We see that, you could say to a certain extent, we see that in politics sometimes, say in the alliance between evangelical Christians and someone such as Trump who espouses a very different set of moral values.

Audience: Hello. With the advent of postmodernism in modern societies, there has also been the problem of moral relativism. And, this can play to the fluidity of identity as a whole, because there are people out there who identify, for instance, as wolves or squirrels, or animals. How do we, as a society, given the issue of moral relativism, accept these people or deny these people their identities?

Svolos: Wolves and squirrels?

Audience: Yes, yes, seriously.

[18] See "A Conversation with President Obama and The Wire Creator David Simon" on the the "Obama White House" YouTube site. Accessed at https://www.youtube.com/watch?v=xWY79JCfhjw on April 3, 2022.

Svolos: You will have to educate me a little bit about this.

Audience: I think it was on TLC, there was this man who identifies as a wolf, and he has a wolf tail. One of his pastimes is going to the ocean and howling. It seems absurd, but there are actual people who live like this, and this is an identity which they identify with on a really personal level, which is something they find that they cannot live without. So, as a society, as I said before, should we accept these people? Because we can, but should we?

Svolos: What do you think?

Audience: I don't think so. I don't think so. I think to some degree, you have to draw a line.

Svolos: But the question would be, "How would we draw the line? Where would we draw the line?" I think we draw the line with violence, if the person kills somebody. If the person breaks the law. But if somebody wants to think he is a wolf, I don't know if that crosses a line. Should I be in trouble for thinking I am a Lacanian psychoanalyst?

(laughter)

Svolos: I mean, maybe I am not a Lacanian psychoanalyst. I think I'm a man, but you know, maybe I have a feminine side that is there. What do you do about the people who are "other"? The people who are different.

Audience: It is kind of tribalistic in a sense, viewing the other side as the other.

Svolos: Yes.

Audience: Maybe we should, instead of viewing them as the other, not necessarily accept them, but interact with them and have experiences with the people we consider the other.

Svolos: That I agree with. Yes, yes! That I completely endorse. Which is, talk to the wolf. No, I mean, as an analyst I would be interested to see the wolf. "Tell me what your life is like as a wolf?"

Renata Texeira: Freud had the Wolf Man and the Rat Man and all the identifications that were so helpful to Freud to recognize and, you know, instead of the name of the father, why not a wolf? It helped them to maybe be balanced.

Svolos: Okay. Though, with Freud's two patients, I think the names Rat Man and Wolf Man were added by Freud and not part of the patients' identities.

I would want to engage in a dialogue with the person, say, who believes he is a wolf. "Why do you think you are a wolf? Why do you like howling at the ocean" and so forth. Yes, yes.

Audience: I would actually like to answer your question. I have a safe blanket that keeps me safe from the world. So, these people with these identities of a wolf, a squirrel, a whatever they want to be—the identity is their safe blanket. It is their way to say, "I am unique even in this world full of people who are also unique, that this makes me special. It makes me extra special. This is a way to protect myself, to continue being unique, and to not merge into a society that wants to constantly keep you under rule."

Svolos: So, that is an answer. And the answer I would say that you gave is, "This is a way that allows the person to live in a world that they find is threatening." By being a wolf, it would be possible, by taking on this identity, I can engage with the world. Late in his work, Lacan states that your symptom, which we often think of as a form of suffering, is ultimately a form of your identity, your symptom is your way of bonding with the world. We bond with other people through our symptom. In the case of the man who puts on the wolf tail and howls at the ocean, perhaps that it is his symptomatic way to engage the world. What is important to recognize is that other people engage the world in symptomatic ways that are not so obvious. My symptom, maybe you in the audience are very smart and can tell what my symptom is, but my symptom, which defines how I engage the world, is not as obvious as that is. And one of the keys, one of the ways of thinking about psychoanalysis, what it is to go through analysis, is you learn about your symptom, you could say. You discover your symptom. Maybe you didn't know about it or maybe you knew this about it, and you discovered this, this, and this, and then, "Well what am I going to do with this?" It is not that you make it want to go away. Whoever made the comment about the blanket is right here, you may not want your symptom to go away. What is the matter with your blanket? I don't think Linus had a problem with his blanket. Your blanket may not be such a bad thing, but what do you do with your blanket? So, the guy, maybe his symptom is a wolf and maybe this is a way that he can work with the world, you know maybe there is another way he could be the wolf and work with the world.

Audience: With his relationship with the body.

Svolos: Yes. Exactly. So, I would say, that is it, and this goes back to the first question about doing without identity. Inasmuch as your identity can have a symptomatic value for you, you may not do without it. Because it could be the way you engage with people, your spouse, your friends, and so forth.

Audience: Good evening. Okay, so aligned with what pretty much everyone has said, I want to rescue something that Lacan talked a lot about, which is the *savoir faire*, what we would call the know-how, which is what basically would come to orient you, to see what you are going to do with that that you are, if you ever figure out the answer to that question. So, this generation generally has a lot of openness to validity. The imaginary is stronger than ever, and we use the symbolic to organize. So, there is a lot that we cannot name that we desperately try to find answers for. So, I believe that it is definitely case by case, you would definitely have to sit down with that wolf man and see what that wolf means to him, why he wants to be a wolf, and why would he identify as a wolf. And that is more of my personal opinion. I would definitely say that we would all search for that know-how and attaining it, I guess, is a mission.

Svolos: Yes. I agree. Sometimes, when people come to an analyst, they are looking for knowledge. Tell me why "X." Why do I think this way? Why do I behave this way? Why can't I stop thinking this? Why do I keep doing this? Why do my relationships always end this way? Why can't I do this at the job? The questions often initially posed are issues of knowledge. "I don't have the knowledge about this. You are an analyst; you must have the knowledge. Give me the knowledge about this." But we don't have the knowledge. We know something, but it is not that that is important. What you said is important. Knowledge in French is *savoir* and *savoir faire* is know-how. That is how we usually translate it. So, it is not knowledge as much as know-how, using something. Knowing how to use it. How do I use my identity? How do I use my symptom? My suffering even. I agree with what you said completely, and I think the point about postmodernity and, if any of you are going to be there tomorrow, I am going to talk a lot about this tomorrow. So, the point about postmodernity, is that the answers are singular, as you put it, case by case. I would argue Freud's answers were a little less singular. I mean, the older psychoanalysis tended to have set answers for things.[19] But, I think in postmodernity, and I think you had mentioned postmodernity too, one of the things we see now in the clinical world, but not just in the clinical world, in the art world and the cultural world, is what is called singularity. For those who follow the great author about postmodernity, Fredric Jameson—who started his work in this area with his 1984 paper on postmodernity—I suggest that you review this wonderful paper he did in 2015 called "The Aesthetics of Singularity," where he talks about singularity in postmodernity, at one point by looking at cuisine and molecular gastronomy and the way people create dishes where the food doesn't look like what it tastes like.[20] The example for him is El Bulli, a famous restaurant in Spain. He also looks at the domain of the economy, in particular, financial derivatives, which are singular financial instruments that are meant to support one particular financial transaction, say, a contract between multiple companies in different countries where the contract is singular, one that could never be generalized. And, then, in the art world, he talks about singularity with his observation that one of the critical developments in the art world is the rise of the installation. Every installation is unique, right? An installation might include a piece of furniture, a rug, a book, a kitchen implement, some video screen. It is a unique, singular artwork. It is not like, say, a novel, where author is writing in the tradition of a certain form of the novel or something like that, but it is a unique piece of art. It is also different from painting—a painter might be identified as from the school of Titian. Each installation is a unique, singular thing. Singularity is true in psychoanalysis as well, in the realm of the psyche. I think there used to be general forms in which the psyche was organized, and now there are these very unique ways that people put their lives together. So, in our world of Lacanian psychoanalysis, certain analysts will present something that they have extracted from their own

---

[19] For greater development on the importance of a historical approach to psychoanalysis, see, for example, Chap. 3 in this book and also chapter 3, "Three Moments, Three Aims," in Thomas Svolos, *The Aims of Analysis: Miami Seminar on the Late Lacan*, New York, Midden Press, 2020; and, also, regarding the impact of this on practice, Thomas Svolos, "History and the Link of the Analytic Act with Civilization," in Chap. 5 in this book.

[20] Fredric Jameson, "Postmodernism; or, the Cultural Logic of Late Capitalism" New *Left Review*, 146, July–August 1984, pages 53–92. Fredric Jameson, "The Aesthetics of Singularity," New *Left Review*, 92, March–April 2015, pages 101–132.

experience of analysis in what are called testimonies. When you read these testimonies, what is interesting to me is they are all very unique, the way the analyst puts their story together and what matters and how they put it together. They are very distinctive. So, I agree with your point about case by case, and I think it is a particular issue right now.

Audience: Right. Freud had it a bit harder. He had to say something for the first time, saying children have sexuality. How do you say that talking about only, for example, I don't know, Tommy, and not talking about children in general? So now, instead of generalizing, I think we are seeing a lot of things that are manifesting individually, and we are having to take a closer look at what it means for each individual, rather than what it means for the individual to go ahead and place it towards society, so the society understands. Because it is the know-how for you and for the other as well.

Audience: Back to where you were saying about different people getting together for a task. What happens when that task is no longer there and there is no need to work together to survive, for example?

Svolos: Then you get a new task. But it may be that groups are temporal, they are limited, time-limited, as we would say in English, time-limited groups. There will always be another task, another possibility of groupings, and it may be that groups come and go in the kind of flux and change in postmodernity. Not that there are not going to be other kinds of groups that form in other, say, more traditional ways, but it could be that this type of a group is the perfect kind of a group in an era where this is going to be more time limited.

In politics, I would say we see this in the flash mobs. I don't know if they do this so much anymore, but there was a period where people would organize protests in what were called flash mobs, say a demonstration about something, and it would spread through social media and people would gather together in a park and, then, it goes away. A time-limited political group, very different from a political party. It is like a happening, or an event.

Alvarez Arango: So, I am going to take your last comments to put a stop now to this time of gathering, which has been delicious, but will come to an end right now. Thank you very much for joining us tonight. I hope to see you again for another task, time-limited also, and enjoy your singular weekend. Thank you.

[Clapping]

Part III

Reading *Civilization and Its Discontents* in the Twenty-First Century

The pandemic led to a proliferation of videoconferencing globally, and the situation was no different in the World Association of Psychoanalysis. The Irish Circle of the Lacanian Orientation, a society of the New Lacanian School, decided to take up Freud's Civilization and Its Discontents *at a moment of great global discontent. After a reading of each chapter of Freud's book, a guest was assigned the task of commenting on the chapter read. My readings of Chaps. 4 and 8 can be found in the next two chapters below. The readings take two very different approaches. In the first, I address the question of the relevance of Freud's text, published in 1930, in the early twenty-first century. While there is much to admire about Freud's approach to linking the personal and the social, there have been significant changes at the levels of both the psyche and society such that the fundamental approach of Freud organized around repression has less impact today. In the second reading, I attempted to put some of our work to use in a series of psychoanalytic interpretations of the global discontent of the first year of the pandemic, during the period of lockdowns and prior to the development of treatments and vaccines. Note that the fate of some of the politicians discussed during these talks, delivered on April 18 and May 30, 2020, has shifted as a result of new reporting on matters associated with the pandemic and other issues.*

3

What Use for *Civilization and Its Discontents* Today?

Abstract In *Civilization and Its Discontents*, Sigmund Freud introduced fundamental psychoanalytic hypotheses about the relationship between social structure and the psyche, including the psychopathology of the neuroses. Freud hypothesized that the repression of sexual and aggressive drives demanded by civilization led to the development of neurosis. While Freud's theory of a relationship of social formations and psychic formations remains invaluable, postmodern society is different in distinctive ways from Freud's Victorian society. Changes in social structure, particularly the dominance of the symbolic order that characterized Freud's era, can be articulated with new psychic structures today and new forms of suffering.

Keywords Sigmund Freud • *Civilization and Its Discontents* • Repressive hypothesis • Neurosis

Florencia Shanahan: For his commentary and I will remind all participants that you can intervene via the chat or raise your hand and we will have plenty of time today for interventions and questions. Thomas . . .

Thomas Svolos: All right, I want to thank Raphael for the reading [of Chapter 4 of *Civilization and Its Discontents*]. I want to offer a special

T. Svolos, *Culture and Politics on the Couch*, The Palgrave Lacan Series,
https://doi.org/10.1007/978-3-031-61365-4_3

thanks to Florencia for the invitation. It probably was fifteen years ago or so that we first met in Europe, I think it would have been at the Rome Congress of the WAP, perhaps, a long time ago. I also want to thank Linda and the other colleagues in the ICLO for this activity and invitation. I want to echo what Florencia said, which is that at a moment of crisis, we are compelled to be creative and invent new things such as this activity, and some of them will probably stick around. I also want to thank the three individuals who preceded me in their discussions and remarks about the first three chapters of Freud's *Civilization and Its Discontents*, which opened up perspectives for me. In fact, I want to start with a question, if I am remembering this correctly, that Roger Litten raised in his discussion, saying something along the lines of: "You know, what is important isn't necessarily what does this text mean, but what use are we going to make of this text. What are we going to do with it?" And that question has really preoccupied me over the last several weeks as we have met and as we have gone about this reading of Freud—and I will have a bit more to say about reading Freud in a few minutes. It led me to reflect on the question in a more general sense of, what use do I make of Freud? What use do I make of Freud in the course of my analysis, for example? What use of Freud do I make in my practice as a psychoanalyst? Obviously, Freud created this practice of psychoanalysis, but that was a long time ago, and as I had thought about this question with regard to my own analysis, I have felt that, more and more, as my experience of analysis has unfolded—and I am reflecting back to working with two psychoanalysts, analysis with the first one began in 1998, so 22 years ago—I know there were Freudian constructions early on, but as I think of the last five years of analysis, Freud is not present so much, thinking of things in Freudian terms, say, making a construction of one sort or another using Freudian language. Rather, it was with Lacan and, in particular for me as I really explored the very final Lacan, that I found some words that allowed me to say something about my analytic experience.

Likewise, when I think of my practice, where does Freud come into play? I will make one observation. Every now and then, I will see someone in my practice that strikes me as, in the phrase I have used to describe this before, as a kind of old-fashioned neurotic, in the sense that the trajectory of the analysis of this particular person goes along the lines in some way or another of something like Freud's Dora case or the Rat Man case. One sees features and the things that have stood out to me in that regard are with some, say, old-fashioned hysterics, the dialectical reversals that Lacan highlighted about how Freud conducted the case, "Oh, I'm a victim, the world is terrible, look at all the bad things that happened to me," and then the moment where you are able to shift something and implicate the subject in his or her existence and suffering.[1] And, those kinds of things, that will happen from time to time. Or, an old-fashioned obsessional where, as with the Rat Man, something about the trajectory of the life story, the path that this person has taken through life, is somehow written in a form of destiny and facts relating to the parental situation, as with the case of the Rat Man.[2] But this is not very often for me that I find cases that play themselves out in this way.

When we think about dreams, Freud describes how he works his dreams in *The Interpretation of Dreams* and also in the case histories. Freud's type of methodical way of working with the dream, as you know, proceeds element by element, with the focus on the day's residues and so forth and so on, is not so much the way I work with dreams now. Also, there is this Freudian aspect of the dream as a deciphering exercise. But, as Angelina Harari emphasized in a talk at a recent Clinical Study Days in Miami, while there is a "meaning dimension" to the dream, for sure, there is also the "use dimension" that comes into play. Then, what about all the other Freudian constructs: Oedipus and Eros and Thanatos and all this other conceptual framework from Freud? I don't find, for myself at least, that that is as useful for me in my practice as it was in the past.

All right, so then for me, this brings up an even simpler question, "What Freud do I read?"

I ask because this was an invitation from Florencia to listen to somebody read the text of Freud. I took the occasion of this seminar to go back and re-read *Civilization and Its Discontents*, each chapter prior to the

[1] Jacques Lacan, "Presentation on Transference," *Écrits: The First Complete Edition in English, op. cit*, pages 176–188.

[2] Jacques Lacan, "The Neurotic's Individual Myth," *Psychoanalytical Quarterly*, Vol. 48, Issue 3, 1970, pages 405–425.

meeting.[3] And, it occurred to me that it has been several years since I sat down and read a longer text of Freud from cover to cover. I cannot honestly remember the last time I sat down and read Freud methodically. I go back to pull quotes and notes from Freud when I am writing something and want to look something up, but I have not sat down with a text like this in a long time. Now, that is not to say I have not read this before, I probably read it a half dozen times along with most of Freud's other works, but most of it was a long time ago. So, it has been an interesting thing for me to go back and re-read Freud. For psychoanalysts maybe of my age, reading Freud is always re-reading Freud. It is what happens as a psychoanalyst when you get older. What Freud do I find compelling? For Lacan, it was very clear: many times, Lacan spoke of his interest in Freud the discoverer of the unconscious and, in particular, his early texts on dreams, jokes, and parapraxes, where he was in the process of creating psychoanalysis, discovering the unconscious. Lacan was often critical of the later Freud, the second topology, and I think some of the metapsychological dimensions, particularly of the later Freud.

But, in preparing for this, I came upon something interesting in Lacan's work. I went back and looked through the seminars to see what Lacan had to say about *Civilization and Its Discontents*, and I came across this reference in *Seminar VII* that I thought was particularly interesting and that, for me, sets the context for this exercise. I believe this might have been the seminar where Lacan discussed *Civilization* more than any other place in his work. I am going to read a small passage, a paragraph, from Lacan on page 6 in the English. "This *Civilization and Its Discontents* that I invite you to get to know, or to re-read in the context of Freud's work, is not just a set of notes. It is not the kind of thing one grants a practitioner or a scientist somewhat indulgently as his way of making an excursion into philosophical inquiry without our giving it all the technical importance one would accord to such a thought coming from someone who considers himself to belong to the category of philosopher. Such a view of this work of Freud's is widespread among psychoanalysts and is definitely to be rejected. *Civilization and Its Discontents* is an indispensable work,

[3] Sigmund Freud, "Civilization and Its Discontents," *The Standard Edition of the Complete Psychological Works of Sigmund Freud*, Vol. 21, London, Hogarth, 1964, pages 59–148.

unsurpassed for an understanding of Freud's thought and the summation of his experience. It illuminates, emphasizes, dissipates the ambiguities of wholly distinct points of the analytic experience and of what our view of man should be."[4] So, what Lacan is saying is that we should not read *Civilization* as a kind of speculative exercise of a quasi-philosophical nature, but we should read it as having something to say about the analytic experience. So, for Lacan, in 1959 at least, he believed that there was something valuable about the psychoanalytic experience in this text.

My question for us is, "Is that still true today?" I am not so sure, and if it is, in what way? For my own sake, I would say this. For me, yes, I agree. The three fundamental texts Lacan frequently referenced about Freud are interesting. But for me, the things that were most compelling about Freud were also the letters to Fliess and the letters to Jung: the correspondence where you can sense Freud grappling with this unknown and trying to make sense of it and working his cases or on institutional issues and describing them to his colleagues in a very pragmatic way. And, I also got that sense reading *Beyond the Pleasure Principle*, where he is confronted with a new phenomenon, and he is really struggling and working on how to make sense of it in the clinical arena. Those are more interesting texts to me. This is not Freud dealing with an intact and complete Other that he will describe, Freud developing a system, but rather Freud facing an Other with a hole in it, a hole in meaning, with which he engages and grapples. I think of these moments in Freud as the most compelling.

But, anyhow, let's take Lacan's advice not to treat this as a philosophical text but a text rather that addresses the psychoanalytic experience. What can we say then along those lines? I would say that one significant thing is that throughout Freud's work, and maybe put together in this text especially clearly, in the development of his theory of the libido, Freud also recognizes that there is a relationship and a connection between the psychic or subjective dimension of the experience of the libido and the social. This, to me, is a fundamental contribution of Freud, which I think it seems clear to me and chapter 4 is maybe as clear as anywhere

[4] Jacques Lacan, *The Seminar of Jacques Lacan: Book VII, The Ethics of Psychoanalysis, 1959–1960*, New York, Norton, 1992, pages 6–7.

else, in the way the whole matter of the libido is organized around the notion of repression. I think the central fact for Freud is that of repression, and it comes through most clearly in the footnotes. I will have something to say about that in a second. This is a signal contribution from Freud.

The other thing that I think is significant is the issue of sexuality really being essentially lawless, to use a Lacanian phrase, or polymorphous to use a Freudian phrase, and that complete satisfaction of sexuality is impossible. The experience of all this is, for Freud, linked to repression. There were references throughout the text to the essential bisexuality of humans, to the polymorphous perversity of sexuality, to use his phrase from an earlier Freudian text. For Freud, all of the lawless, original sexuality of humans gets repressed and channeled (he uses this word channeled) through the existence of civilization. What he then does, and I will say something about this in a second thought that I think is curious, is he hypothesizes an existence of a moment where that was not true. So, if we think about his repressive hypothesis, the hypothesis of repression supposes a moment prior to civilization where sexuality was utopianly wonderful and perfect and people could pursue their polymorphous, bisexual interests, and so forth. I am not necessarily convinced.

What about this issue of civilization? Veronique Voruz made a number of comments in an earlier session of this reading seminar that I endorse completely. Veronique noted that Freud's civilization, first of all, is clearly not our own. We are in a different civilization. And Veronique made a comment, I hope I can remember it precisely, that we are no longer in the so-called oppressive time of the Victorian Age. We are in a different era. We have new family structures. We have new forms of sexuality that are being explored and are no longer suppressed in the way that they were. The whole social attitude towards sexuality has changed and, as you may be aware, Lacan has taken a number of different approaches to some of the Freudian hypotheses that I will not go into in detail but, for example, Lacan had his own hypothesis with regard to the drive theory and the notion of Eros and Thanatos. Lacan was one of the few analysts at that moment who accepted the notion of the death drive, but I believe that his contribution in saying that, in essence, every drive includes the death drive, takes us out of the realm of the binary into something new and different. Or, take Freud's belief that the drives are always repressed, and the libido is always repressed. That is not so always for Lacan. Rather, Lacan notes that the drive always finds satisfaction. By the end of his work, Lacan states that the subject is always happy, whether it is happy, in Freudian terms, in an aim-directed or in an aim-inhibited way, it doesn't matter, because the drive always finds satisfaction.[5]

I want to make some more general comments about *Civilization and Its Discontents*, before I say a few specific things about chapter 4. Freud's discursive world is no longer ours. Let us take, for example, some of the passing comments Freud makes. For example, in addition to what he says about libidinal energy and repression, he also talks about science. Freud's science has nothing to do with how we look at science now, certainly a Lacanian view of science. Freud was a positivist. He was a Comtean in his approach, and he believed that there was going to be gradual and gradual progress in discovering things and at some point, I cannot remember in which text he talked about it, he stated that science will eventually even tackle the mind and biology will figure it all out. This is a view of science that has no relationship with what Lacan has to say about Galileo and the development of modern science and the role of letters and so forth.[6] Lacan's view of science is completely different.

If you go back and read Freud's text on art, you will read about great art, great men: Freud pulls these things out of art, such as eternal truths and so forth and so on. But for me, one of the most interesting things that Lacan had to say about art was in his work *Homage to Marguerite Duras*, where he talks about how the artist in a sense precedes the psychoanalyst in discovering things to say about what is happening in the world, which is a radically different way of thinking about how we might use art in psychoanalysis.[7]

---

[5] See, for example, Jacques Lacan, *Television: A Challenge to the Psychoanalytic Establishment*, Norton, 1990, page 22.

[6] Jacques Lacan, *The Seminar of Jacques Lacan: Book XX: Encore (1972–1973)*, New York, W. W. Norton, 1998.

[7] Jacques Lacan, "Homage to Marguerite Duras, on *Le ravissement de Lol V. Stein," Duras by Duras*, San Francisco, City Light Books, 1987, pages 123–124.

And at the same time, Freud's notion of beauty bears no relationship with Lacan's, and I do not want to go into the detail with what Lacan had to say about beauty, for example in the Ethics Seminar.

All right, what about this chapter? My first question is, "What in the world do we call this? What do we call this kind of speculation?" Because it is speculation, for me, about the past. It is not archeology, because archeology implies the study of real objects from the past. I think we could characterize this as a kind of mythology. Lacan, if I recall correctly in *Seminar XVII*, talks about Freud spinning myths. And, this is a kind of myth that Freud is developing in this chapter. There is something that is unknown, and, in fact, it is completely unknowable. We will never know what happened in the prehistoric era that Freud is spinning these tales about. And so, in response to an unknown, we create stories that are like myths or fantasies, but as myths are social phenomenon, this is more like a fantasy on Freud's part, I think, of what happened. What is interesting to me about it is that it is a fantasy that implies the existence of a time when the sexual relation was possible. Lacan talks about the non-rapport, the sexual non-rapport. What Freud is creating is a moment when he believed that there existed a sexual rapport in humanity. I believe that this says probably more about Freud than it does about what happened, say, 5000 or 10,000 years ago in prehistoric human history. It reminds me of comments Lacan makes in *Seminar XX* where he talks about prescientific or premodern knowledge always including an inscription of the sexual bond. In this sense, Freud is hypothesizing an inscription of the sexual bond at a moment in time (based on his scientific views that are premodern, in the Lacanian sense).

And, he does this most clearly in the footnotes. I asked Raphael if it would be acceptable to read the footnotes, because it is in the footnotes that he has some of the most interesting things to say and, particularly, the final footnote. I want to reference several specific sentences and make a few comments about them, but I think the existence of these almost mini-essays in the footnotes is very interesting, and they reminded me of a comment, which I am going to read in a second, that Fred Jameson made about the function of footnotes in Adorno's *Philosophy of New Music*. Jameson's comment is that

> This should not, however, be taken as evidence for the presence of two alternating and imperfectly assimilated modes of dialectal thought in Adorno's work. There, on the contrary, an almost physical cause may be said to account for the structural peculiarity of the text in question, which is neither more nor less than a complete footnote: and the abundance, as well as the stylistic and philosophical quality, of the footnotes to *Philosophy of the New Music* is itself "no accident" and has symptomatic value. The footnote in this context may indeed be thought of as a small but autonomous form, with its own inner laws and conventions and its own determinate relationship to the larger form which governs it—something on the order of the moral of a fable or the various types of digressions, which flourished within the nineteenth century novel. In the present instance, the footnote as a lyrical form allows Adorno a momentary release from the inexorable logic of the material under study in the main text, permitting him to shift to other dimensions, to the infrastructure as well as to the wider horizons of historical speculation. The very limits of the footnote (it must be short, it must be complete) allow the release of intellectual energies, in that they serve as check on a speculative tendency that might otherwise run wild, on what we will later describes as the proliferation of "theories of history." The footnote as such, therefore, designates a moment in which systematic philosophizing and the empirical study of concrete phenomena are both false in themselves; in which living thought, squeezed out from between them, pursues its fitful existence in the small print at the bottom of the page.[8]

These two long footnotes, footnote 1 and footnote 3, are significant, and I want to make a few comments about them. One is in the first footnote where Freud develops this whole notion of the importance of the shift from olfactory to visual sexual excitation and the impact of that on anal eroticism that all occurred with the movement to an upright stature in gait, all of which he links to the focus on cleanliness. For me, this is pure speculation on Freud's part. We will never know this, and when I thought about this particular hypothesis of Freud's in the context of the question I raised at the beginning—"What use do we make of this?"—I cannot find any use for this other than to say something about Freud

[8] Fredric Jameson, *Marxism and Form: Twentieth-Century Dialectical Theories of Literature*, Princeton, Princeton University Press, 1971, page 9.

perhaps. As I stated before, I think, in a sense, we can think of this as Freud's fantasy and worthy of analysis.

However, in the third footnote, there is something very interesting, several interesting comments. Freud discusses the issue of essential bisexuality. He talks about how anatomy can distinguish between the sexes, but not psychology. He evokes the traditional Greek notion of active and passive for male and female, and then he makes a comment that I think is Freud at his best. He says, "The theory," and this is a quote. I will read it from the newer Penguin translation, which is a little easier to read, less wooden in style. They are a little more literary for today's time. Freud says, "The theory of bisexuality is still shrouded in obscurity, and the fact that it has not been connected with that of the drives is bound to strike us as a serious flaw in psychoanalysis."[9] To me, this is Freud at his best, when he is looking at a problem, and he recognizes this and describes it in a very candid way. And what is most interesting to me about that particular quote of Freud's is that he alludes to some of the very points that Lacan, I think, tries to develop through his work with the notion of the object *a*, with the formulas of sexuation that he develops in *Seminars XIX* and *XX*, and with his attempt to find different ways to articulate what we might talk about as the symbolic and the real. Freud sees that this is a problem, how to develop this, and my argument would be that in Lacan's work, we see an attempt to address this very deficit that Freud very honestly speaks to in the footnote.

Then, finally, this comment from the final footnote where Freud says, "The ultimate root of the sexual oppression that accompanies cultural progress would seem to be the organic defense of the new way of life ushered in by man's adoption of an upright gait, against his earlier animal existence."[10] Throughout the text and in this particular footnote, including in this passage, Freud alludes to the fundamental importance of repression on civilization, in addition to these speculations about a time when it did not exist.

I want to suggest if we think about the question of what use do we make of this fundamental hypothesis about civilization, it is that we do

[9] Sigmund Freud, *Civilization and Its Discontents*, New York, Penguin Classics, 2002, pages 62–63.
[10] Sigmund Freud, *Ibid.*, pages 63–64.

not make much use of it now or, let's put it this way, if we follow Jacques-Alain Miller's work, we no longer think about psychoanalysis today so much from the vantage point of repression. I am sure many of you have read these texts that were translated in *The Lacanian Review* two years ago, "The Space of a Lapsus" and "The Space of a Hallucination."[11] In those very critical seminars of Miller, he speaks about how, in the late Lacan, we reach a perspective where we are no longer building psychoanalysis on the basis of repression. Miller constructs his argument from several things, drawing from Freud's Wolf Man case and the episode of the severed finger and drawing from Lacan's comment on Hyppolite's comments on Freud's negation. Miller develops a hypothesis that the psychoanalysis that we create now, at the moment of the final Lacan, is not a psychoanalysis based on repression and the return of the repressed in unconscious formations and so forth, but rather on the hallucination and the existence in the analytic experience of pieces of the real that are not subject to the old formulas of laws of repression and so forth.

Shanahan: I think, Tom, that is a point that I would like to highlight and maybe for the discussion, this way of formulating what do we build psychoanalysis on today? It seems to me very important.

Svolos: And, this was my final point, in fact. So, I am done, but in concluding, I want to emphasize this: for me, that *Civilization* is a beautiful text to read because it highlights the difference between how Freud built psychoanalysis and how many people are using it today, which is in a different way. So, with that, I will turn the microphone over to other people.

Shanahan: Okay. Thank you very much, Thomas, we have time to engage our participants and also Raphael and also our guest commentators who can be here today with us. There are a couple of questions already that maybe we could start with, but we have two raised hands. Raphael, would you like to intervene?

Raphael Montague: Yes, okay. There are a number of things that occurred to me in respect to Thomas' commentary. I think at this point

[11] Jacques-Alain Miller, "The Space of a Lapsus," *The Lacanian Review*, #6, Fall 2018, page 62–81. Jacques-Alain Miller, "The Space of a Hallucination," *The Lacanian Review*, #6, Fall 2018, page 82–108.

in time in Freud's writing, it is 1929, isn't it? It is the year of the Great Depression, which our current circumstance have been likened to, or at least the proposed economic effect of this crisis we have created via a virus. I think at this point in time of Freud's work, yes, he is a logical positivist, but I think his belief in that is wavering. I think at this stage in his work, he does not believe that logical positivism is going to come to fruition in the way that the fathers of the Enlightenment had supposed: that given knowledge, technology, education, universities, advanced mathematics, advanced science, man was going to produce a civilization without discontent. I do not think Freud believes that at this point in time. Now, what do you do if you have built your career, in a certain sense, as a medical professional . . . [inaudible] what do you do? Well, you create a myth, which is a construction in analysis essentially. Now, we are going to be publishing, digitally publishing, a very special issue of *Scriobh*, which is a periodic newsletter of the Irish Circle of Lacanian Orientation. I am not going to give the game away on that.

Shanahan: No, because it is an invention that has not been announced yet.

*Montague***:** It has not been announced yet? Okay, well, you can take it as announced there.

Shanahan: Exactly.

*Montague***:** So, what I am going to do is say something about what it is that Lacan is doing with Freud. You can see in the "Preface to the English Language Edition of *Seminar XI*," which I think is published in English in 1977, so it was quite late in Lacan's career. He adds this preface, what he says is probably the most dense three pages of writing anybody has ever produced. It says an awful lot, but what he says in respect to reading and re-reading Freud is very interesting, that for him, in terms of singularity, he thought the trauma produced in reading Freud was Lacan's real. That is essentially what he says and, in this particular digital issue that we are going to publish, I am going to read one quote from a text that is in it. I am not going to say anything other than that, other than read, I am not going to give the game away. But I want to read this particular quote because it really sums up re-reading Freud in the Lacanian orientation, in the fullness of that. So, I quote, "Far from making one concept concord with another, what is at stake is the reconstruction of the point of the real to which those concepts respond and therefore, also the reconstruction of the transformation that this produces."[12] That is what Lacan is doing when he is reading Freud. You see, he is not looking to make the whole thing hang together, he is looking to identify the points of failure or rupture, the things Freud could not get his head around with respect to the sexual relation, for example. Things Freud could not get his head around with respect to logical positivism as a failed paradigm. So, I think that is very important in re-reading these texts. It is a very good reason to do it. We are reconstructing something, a point of the real, of an impossibility, something that does not work. It did not work in Freud's time, and it does not work today. I think we are going to see that down the line with respect to gender fluidity as a solution to binary. We are going to see that is going to come to its limit point at some stage also, and Freud is remarkably prescient in this particular chapter. He gives a very good description of what is going to happen and what did happen with respect to sexuality from, you know, 1929 up to 2019, over a 90-year period, remarkably prescient. Yes, monogamy is going to fail as a societal structure. Different modes of sexual enjoyment come to the fore. This binary of masculine/feminine is going to be exposed as not working for us and so on. So, I think he is remarkably prescient with respect to his social commentary. Also, what he is grappling with, I think, you see there is a very important fragment of a sentence where he talks about the neurotics and all the rest. He is grappling with, and this is the last thing I am going to say, I think. He is grappling with as a logical positivist that there is no normal. The statistical mean that would provide the benchmark for normality is just that, and there is nothing that it refers to. So, basically, he has gone to the well, and the well is empty, and now he is upset.

Shanahan: Thank you very much, Raphael. Very interesting comments and we have Gustavo Dessal and Roger Litten who are going to have their mics open. First Gustavo, then Roger. Gustavo, good morning.

Gustavo Dessal: Good morning. Hi everybody. Hello Raphael and Thomas. I thank you very much for your reading and comments. Thomas, I find that your initial questions are very interesting, "What is the use of

[12] Interview with Leonardo Gorostiza, "The Lacanian Orientation—*Clarifying the Abruptness of the Real*," *Scríobh*, #7, May 2020, page 3.

this text today?" And between the lines, you asked "what is the use of Freud today?" Well, I think it is also a question of taste. In my experience, I could not skip Freud in order to perform my own practice. I would like to, if you allow me a few minutes, I would like to pinpoint at least three, in my opinion, three outstanding observations in this text. In this sense, I find them very, very Lacanian.

One has already been mentioned that you indicated to us: the footnote where Freud poses that the biological difference between maleness and femaleness is clear while very difficult to establish at the psychological level and, in such a way, of course, we need Lacan to find this. If not, it would have been impossible. But, with Lacan, we can say that Freud has, well let's say a naïve anticipation of what becomes in Lacan, the thesis of the sexual non-rapport.

The second point is the idea that, for example, heterosexuality as the sexual norm is something abusive, something that imposes, he says, a single kind of sexual life for everybody. I think this is bold. This is astonishing in that moment because Freud adds, "In doing so all civilization commits an injustice that is the source of suffering and symptoms." Because, I think that the text is, as you say, organized on the basis of repression, but also on the basis of the return of the repressed. We must not forget that.

And the third point: even the prototypical satisfaction admitted by civilization is submitted to forced restrictions, but at the same time, Freud thinks that satisfaction is impaired not only by external restrictions, and this is very up to date. The idea that what spoils satisfaction is known only as the effect of regression. That is, something internal in the way satisfaction is built up. This is a very Lacanian point. For example, I agree with you absolutely that we have to get this as a myth, that is important in the footnote. Especially the footnote concerning, let me say it this way, concerning shit. The relationship between shit and civilization. The way civilization teaches us to deal with shit and the way that dealing is at the same time impossible because shit returns every time. And this is very useful in our clinic because this can be very funny, for instance. We are prone to admit that the other's shit smells very badly. That is a way the analysand tends to state, to say that in general: it is the other's shit that smells very badly. One of the most important conditions to begin to shift that is to make the subject begin to think that maybe he has to be aware of the way his own or her own shit stinks. That is all, thank you.

Shanahan: Thank you, Gustavo. Very interesting, and there were two questions that go back to the point of our relationship to our own shit, to say it like that. But, we will come back to those questions in a minute. Roger, welcome.

Roger Litten: Hello everyone. Thank you, Raphael and Thomas for all your provocative comments and questions that open up a space where we can think in, say, 3D about some of the things that are going on. Quite frankly, for this whole project where we hear the text that normally we would read in silence, I am astonished by what we hear by reading it aloud. There is something about the cultural history of reading and writing, how the articulation between reading, writing, speaking, and hearing has changed over the years, and let's say digital technology of writing where it shifts between the hearing and the reading. So, certainly hearing something read aloud, to some extent we could say that our psychic anteriority comes from learning to read silently whereas before, reading aloud was all in the monasteries and was always a community activity. There was one text and multiple, multiple auditors. This is the political realm of the scribes and then of the readers and the priests in civilization, who were precisely the masters of the text, all the way to Guttenberg and Luther. Guttenberg made the text multiple, and Luther opened up direct access to the text for each one of us, not having to go via the priestly order, the masters of the book. So, now we have a direct access to the text, each one of us, in the reading, but it does not mean that something has not shifted. And in the fifteenth century, we went through a revolution in printing in our relation to the text, which led to a religious revolution with the reformation and the scientific revolution, and we can presume that 500 years later, we are going through another digital revolution of an equivalent magnitude, shall we say, with the digital revolution where all the pieces are moving around and whatever the incidental occurrences that we have to deal with, we are seeing a shifting of the tectonic plates including all three coordinates of subjectivity. But that is about hearing the text aloud for a change rather than each one of us in our monistic cell reading in silence in the anteriority of our unconscious. That is not what I was going to say. That was the preamble.

I have just another couple of comments that I just want to add. Because it was provoked by some of the things that Thomas said more generally about what role for Freud now and what role for this text, how do we take on this text, and then more specifically about that fantastic footnote that we were not going to read because a footnote is not obviously part of the text. What is the statement between the text and the footnote? In this case, it turns out that the footnote might be the key to certainly the whole chapter, if not to the whole text. On the question of what use Freud and this argument, which is not an early Freud, this is at the end of Freud's work, towards the end of his life, a substantial clinical immersion in the unconscious, why is he still so tied, shall we say, to these mythical speculations of origins in the series of the father, *Totem and Taboo*, Oedipus, all the myths including shall we say the myth of the drive? It is really striking to hear Lacan say, not just the death drive, as Thomas said, which he has no use for, but the drive itself as the Freudian mythology. How do you grasp, what does it mean to put all the drives under the category of Freudian mythology unless it helps us to bring into focus that the one thing that is not mythology is castration? So, the true Freudian discovery is the role of castration and the mythology of the drives then elaborated around that question of castration, including the death drive elaborated in relation to that notion of castration. An absolutely contemporary question is how do we see the death drive played out today, in which modalities around the persistent real of castration, and whether it takes the form of the non-rapport?

Shanahan: I think it would be interesting to let Thomas maybe speak to that point.

Svolos: It would be. I don't know what I would have to say to that, because I think we would have to first develop the question of the context. Thank you, Roger. It is a great point to make. But, in the context of civilization, where does castration fit in? So, if we think about the Freudian laws of repression and the return of the repressed and so forth, does castration fit in that? Does castration fit in what we could call the sociological hypothesis? You know, for Freud sometimes it seems to do that. What Lacan makes of it, I think, is totally different. I mean, I think, I would be curious if, Roger, you asked the question, if you might have an answer to it because it seems to me that with Lacan, it does not come into play in the issue of repression and the return of the repressed and so forth. It does not come into play as a societal phenomenon. You know, Lacan always makes fun of a certain reading of castration, the "Papa's going to cut off your little wee-wee" notion of castration. But, for Lacan, I think it is a fact of language.

Shanahan: In a way, Thomas, this can be linked to this point you made about what do we build psychoanalysis on today? Because there is no doubt, and I think perhaps Roger was pointing towards that as well, that for the practice that psychoanalysis is, for the practice as defined by Lacan as a way of intervening in the real or on the real by means of the symbolic. There is no doubt that clinically we face an era where the unconscious as such and where desire as an effect of castration does not present itself as evident or as obvious in our everyday clinic. And that in any case, that brings us back to what was discussed by some of our commentators before, which is the dialectic—or lack of—between the place of the ideal, the place of the symbolic, and the predominance of the object. So, castration is a name for what Lacan calls the divided subject and what Gustavo pointed towards was that there is an operation that is no longer a given because of certain changes in our world. It is no longer a given that there is a relationship of the subject to himself that is based on the division that castration installs. That brings about for us the responsibility to question and elaborate what we build psychoanalysis on if it is not the case that we think psychoanalysis is a theory that we impose, but rather that we go—as Freud did—and listen to the people who come to us. If it is the latter, then I think this discussion finds its proper place.

So, I am going to give the voice to some of the questions in the chat. We have still some time, about 20 to 25 minutes, but we have at least five questions. The first one is "How should we understand the fact that it is becoming more popular for people to watch live streaming of feces eating when it is separated from the sense of smell? From my research, this feces eating has not much to do with eating feces as eroticism or masochism, but the public exhibition of being recognized as someone who eats feces. What are your thoughts on the livestreaming of feces eating considering that it is related to anal eroticism but different from it?" I did not know this existed.

Svolos: I did not know it existed either, but I guess my first response, and I think Florencia alluded to it, or maybe it was in the question itself. I think the issue is, "Does watching someone eating feces have anything to do with anal eroticism?" That is not obvious to me at all. I mean it could be something else that is in play. And you don't know what it is. And I don't think that an analyst can speak about it without the feces eater being under transference. You would need an analysand in front of you, on the couch, in a chair, talking about their interest in making or watching such videos to be able to make sense of it, because the interesting thing to me is that if we are going to use this old drive language, that just because feces is involved does not necessarily mean it has anything to do with the anal drive.

The specific drive in play in a repetition is not always clear. I give a very personal example for me, that I spoke about, that for me I struggled with overeating and, in my work with my first analyst, it was all talking about it in terms of the oral drive, and it turns out it had nothing to do with that. It had to do with something else, and a completely different drive.[13] So, the mistake you can make in practice is thinking that feces necessarily has to do with anal drive. It may not have to do with that at all. The anal drive for Freud is classically linked to the obsessional, along with the preoccupation of thought and things like that that—all of which we think of as the classical Freudian description of obsessional neuroses. But, approaching this from Lacan's perspective, there is this wonderful comment from Lacan in *Seminar XXIII*, that has been developed by Jacques-Alain Miller and by Éric Laurent, where the issue often with the obsessional neurosis now is to tear the obsessional away from his fascination with the gaze.[14] This is a very different way of thinking about obsessional neurosis from the Freudian perspective. So, for me, it is an interesting question, but I would want to talk with somebody who is interested in making or watching such live streams and then you could figure out what it is about.

[13] Thomas Svolos, Chapter 4, "An Interpretation That Hit the Mark," *The Aims of Analysis: Miami Seminar on the Late Lacan*, *Op. cit.*, pages 125–156.

[14] Jacques Lacan, *The Seminar of Jacques Lacan: Book XXIII: The Sinthome (1975–1976)*, Cambridge, Polity, 2016, page 9. For an elaboration of this, see also the interview with Éric Laurent, "The Unconscious and the Body Event," *The Lacanian Review*, #1, Spring 2016, page 181.

Shanahan: Thank you. The second question is "We are accustomed to say that every human being displays both male and female instincts, attributes. Could you comment on this in association with *Seminar XX*, *Encore*, and the formulas of sexuation?" We would need a year's seminar to address this!

Svolos: (laughter) Yes, it would be a big comment but let me start with a comment about Freud. I agree with Gustavo, let me just add as I do not want my comments to be taken the wrong way: Freud is absolutely essential for a psychoanalyst. I assert that a psychoanalyst has to read Freud and know Freud's work. It would be very difficult to read Lacan if you had not read Freud first, and I agree with the comments made by Gustavo and the interesting remark from Raphael about this subject, but I find that this notion of Freud's about the essential bisexuality of the human experience is picked up by Lacan and who, you could say following Gustavo's comments here, maybe in a sense was able to see even further than Freud about the direction maybe where this was going.

To give a very simple answer to the question: you could think of male and female, to use this term we use sometimes, as semblants. It is a little fiction we make that can be very fluid, but, at the same time, I think what Lacan was interested in trying to determine is if there was some way you could also describe sexuation as a logic that had some connection, say, with *jouissance* or the different ways of approaching the real. That is a very, very different matter—to define sexuation not on the basis of semblant or identity or even universal law, but on the basis of the libido or *jouissance*.[15] So, there are two ways I think I would approach the answer, which I am not going to elaborate on now, because Florencia is right, it would be a long discussion, but one would be to think of it from the standpoint of a *sinthome*, a logical way of taking hold of the real, a way of dealing with *jouissance*, and the other would be at the level of a semblant or a kind of a fiction that one would make of oneself. I think Freud recognized the problem in the quote that I gave from the footnote, and Lacan developed some interesting ways of approaching the problem.

---

[15] See Marie-Hélène Brousse, *The Feminine: A Mode of Jouissance*, New York, Lacanian Press, 2022, for just such an elaboration.

Shanahan: The next question comes from Rik Loose in Dublin whom you know and whom you had in that corner of the world where you live.

Svolos: Yes. We know Rik through meetings and his written work on addiction, and he also was invited to speak in the United States about addiction in 2006, if I recall correctly.

Shanahan: Rik asks, "Freud believed in the progress of science and in a sense, as you mentioned, also in the sexual rapport. However, is this not in a way contradicted, which I think is also part of Freud's way of thinking, by the second to last sentence on page 105." That second to last sentence on page 105 says, "One is probably justified in assuming that its importance as a source of feeling of happiness, and therefore in the fulfilment of our aim in life, has sensibly diminished."[16] Talking about . . .

Svolos: Yes, and the one following maybe was the one he was alluding to, "Now and then one seems to realize that it is not just the pressure of civilization, but that something inherent in the function itself that denies us total satisfaction."[17] And, I believe that is the sentence that Gustavo alluded to as well in his comment. I would agree, and I think to pick up maybe on Gustavo's comment, Rik's question, and also to say a thing about what Raphael said: it seems to me that I do not know that Freud's position on science wavered. I would say that Freud's belief perhaps in progress certainly changed over the course of his life. Freud, I believe, is probably more pessimistic later in his life and in his practice than he was at the beginning. There was a moment, if you think about it in terms of the history of psychoanalysis, I think there was a moment when Freud believed that if you could release the repressed, you might say, if you could decipher the symptom and release the repressed and allow it to get it out in the open, that a psychoanalysis would have positive effects. There was an optimism early in his practice that got tampered down over the course of, I don't know, a decade or something, and led in part to *Beyond the Pleasure Principle*. So, I would say about psychoanalysis itself, Freud became gradually more pessimistic with time about psychoanalysis.

Montague: I am going to jump back in here, Thomas, if I could.

---

[16] Sigmund Freud, "Civilization and Its Discontents," *The Standard Edition of the Complete Psychological Works of Sigmund Freud, op. cit.*, page 105.

[17] *Ibid.*

Svolos: Yes, yes.

Montague: So, we are talking about, in a sense, differences between Freud and Lacan, and, at a certain point in Freud's work, he says the following, "When we study reactions to early traumas, we are quite often surprised to find that they are not strictly limited to what the subject himself has really experienced but diverge from it in a way, which fits in much better with the model of a phylogenetic event and, in general, can only be explained by such an influence. The behavior of neurotic children towards their parents in the Oedipus and castration complex abounds in such reaction, which seems unjustified in the individual case and only becomes intelligible phylogenetically—by their connection with the experience of earlier generations."[18] So, you see, this is why I love Freud. He questions his own theory, the whole lot of it and says, "It is not hanging together for me." I think something else here, and this is the point of the trauma that Lacan comes to when we are talking about the castration complex where [inaudible] this Freudian phylogenetic event while in the Lacanian parlance, we are talking about castration as a facet of language. So, each one is subject to this facet but in terms of singularity, in terms of the effect of it. It is the production of singularity in respect to the Freudian symptom, which is already a linguistic construct in relation to the body and in relation to what Lacan will come to talk about in terms of the body as an enjoying substance, which is not at all as the theory about repression and drive.

Svolos: Yes.

Shanahan: Thank you, Raphael. There is another question in the chat: "A question that has bothered me for a while: the olfactory orifice is the only one in the body that is not associated with a drive—oral, anal, genital, scopic, or invocatory. Along with the auditory, it is the only other orifice that cannot be closed by the body. After listening to Raphael read this chapter where the olfactory is elevated to an originary place, I wonder if this is more than arbitrary, mere oversight on Freud and Lacan's part?" Very interesting question.

[18] Sigmund Freud, "Moses and Monotheism," *The Standard Edition of the Complete Psychological Works of Sigmund Freud*, Vol. 23, 1964, London, Hogarth, page 99.

Svolos: It is interesting. I like that question. I would say, I occasionally will hear people talk about smells but not that often. So, if you think about in your practice, is it something we encounter often? I have encountered it. I have never thought of theorizing the issue. I guess one response that I would have would be that it depends on whether or not the oral drive is strictly conceptualized from the perspective of nurture and eating and intake and what not, as you know, everything having to do with taste associated with oral drive is largely olfactory. This is because we do not taste in the mouth, we taste in the nose. If I recall, the only things you sense in the mouth itself are sweetness and acidity and I think salinity and bitterness. There are a few things that are sensed in the tongue but everything else with regard to aromas has to do with the retro-nasal passage. But, it is not something that I seemed to have encountered that much in my practice. I would be curious about others. I can think of at least one case presentation I heard a long time ago that was entirely built around some olfactory symptoms associated with an analysand and honestly, I do not remember the details other than the fact that the person who presented it offered some kind of hypothesis about this.

Shanahan: It is very interesting, for example, how everything is taken in the classification and invention of new allegedly medical categories, and you can see this on these awful TV programs that have been there for the last ten years mostly, which have to do with building a TV program around this kind of phenomenon. Whether it is things that people do with their bodies or with their house or . . . in the medical sphere, there has been a proliferation of diagnoses of newly invented, if you like, conditions that have to do notably with subjective experiences with regards to the senses. That is not, I agree with you, Thomas, this is not our clinic, this is not . . . to go back to the point. We do not build psychoanalysis on these modifications of general discourses, but we nevertheless take them into account, and we are very attentive to how, to put it in Lacan's terms in *Seminar XIX*, how bodies are captured by discourse. And also, in relation to that . . .

Svolos: One thing quickly: I can think of some schizophrenics I have taken care of over the years who have talked about sometimes the things they smell. He is right. This was from a long time ago, so . . .

Shanahan: Yes, but it is again, because for us, the body is not a given and the experience that a speaking being can construct with regards to his body, it is not enough to have organs for them to be organs. I was very flabbergasted by some consequences to try to illustrate this. The consequences that the alleged scientific discoveries or announcements by so-called science, which 99% of the time are stupid by science, you know, this new study discovered this and that. . . . Either they are complete tautologies such as the headline that notes, "Harvard study demonstrates that early experiences are important for the future," things like that, or they are quite amusing. For example, the effect of this announcement of how "men's balls, I'm sorry, testicles have tastebuds." So, what that produced was a string of YouTubers and people that live their lives in this TikTok, or I don't know what these worlds are, by men dipping their testicles in food, notably peanut butter for some reason, to verify this. So, you see, you have something that comes as a discovery, as a supposedly scientifically structured discourse (it is in fact scientificism), and then, the question of how that is taken up by concrete subjects or communities, and, of course, we cannot speak to that in the way that we build our clinic from the singular speech of each analysand. I thought it was interesting.

I lost complete track of where we are. Neus Carbonell says, "To my understanding, smells form part of the anal drive, it is present often in the clinic of psychosis but also in hysteria."

Another note in the chat: "The sensory disorders are very commonly diagnosed as such in the case of autistic children. They more and more tend to consider them as olfactive and other sensory disorders." I think perhaps we can open the mic to Neus as well there because this would be an aspect of the clinic that she would for sure have something to contribute to. I have not thought of this. I really thank all participants for taking this angle with your comments, because it is true that in the so-called epidemic of diagnosis of autistic spectrum and in the therapies proposed for them, the question of the senses and the sensory experience is at the foreground and, in a way, the question would be whether this way of thinking about the body in terms of the drives with Freud, I am sticking to this text that we are working on, can be useful for something in that respect. Neus?

Neus Carbonell: Hi. Thank you, Thomas, for your talk today. Thank you, Raphael, for the reading. It has been really enlightening. It is true that autistic children smell a lot. You can see them smelling objects, their own hands. I can think of autistic children that play with tablets and the first thing they do when they pick up the tablet is to smell it. In autism, we do not find the drive constructed as such because jouissance has not been regulated by the signifier. Therefore, instead of speaking of sensory disorders, psychoanalysis considers the difficulties that the autistic has with the body and its satisfaction as an effect of a non-regulated jouissance.

Svolos: There is an other side of the question about that. Would it also align with this phenomenon of the schizophrenics that I can remember from a long time ago in the hospital, some of them had what we would think of then as olfactory hallucinations? They would have these olfactory experiences that functioned like hallucinations. They were something of the real that was not contained in any way, and I remember seeing this maybe just a couple times, but these were generally people in the midst of a psychosis. It was a very troubling experience for them.

Shanahan: But Raphael had made the point before that the smell takes on its significance in relation to either the real or the Other and then you have a way to organize this according to whether a circuit for the drive has been constructed or not, which in a way, tautologically, allows us to show very well how the question of what do we build psychoanalysis on today is not separate from the question of how does each subject builds his own experience as a subject—his world and what does he build it on. So, I think this has been a really, really wonderful meeting. I want to thank everybody and especially Tom and Raphael. Thank you so much for your work today and for sharing your reading, your experience. Thank you to everybody who was there. It is great to have you. We are halfway through this seminar, believe it or not. This is our fourth meeting of eight. Next week, we will welcome Susan McFeely and Roger Litten and I would like to maybe say goodbye. Thank you and see you next Saturday. Bye everyone.

4

Seven Psychoanalytic Hypotheses on the Pandemic Discontent

Abstract Freud characterized the role of society as providing security for its citizens, along with his fundamental articulation of the repressive hypothesis—that society demands the repression of certain sexual and aggressive drives—which he linked with the development of the neurotic form of human suffering. The global response to the pandemic, from the vantage point of summer 2020, was quite varied. Psychoanalytic formulations provided a different lens through which to read in 2020 the heterogeneity of pandemic responses on the part of government and society in general. The Freudian model of the society as the protector of its citizens was evident, most clearly in New Zealand and, in Europe, with Angela Merkel, two female leaders. A different model of structuring societal response was formulated, especially among some in the United States, based on hatred, the negative identification of the virus as an external threat. The loss of a place of a single, universal master that had some dominant role in society—most clearly in the position of Emperor—was replaced with a swarm of figures wanting to take the role of master, as was also seen in the United States. The absence of a symbolic father was also evident in the nostalgia in some countries for a strong man to take the helm. Others turned to the Discourse of the University—to a committee of experts—to take the helm. Another response was aligned with the Discourse of the Capitalist and the need to keep money and labor and

T. Svolos, *Culture and Politics on the Couch*, The Palgrave Lacan Series,
https://doi.org/10.1007/978-3-031-61365-4_4

production circulating. And, finally, without symbolic moorings, the United States also experienced a certain disorganization manifested in the pursuit of diverse libidinal aims.

Keywords Pandemic response • Discourse of the Master • Discourse of the University • Discourse of the Capitalist • Discourse of the Analyst

Florencia Shanahan: Okay, thank you very much, Linda [for the reading of Chapter 8 of *Civilization and Its Discontents*]. It resonates with many of the attempts we are doing to put words on the current state of the world, I am sure, for many of you. So, I will now hand over to Thomas, and we look forward to his commentary.

Thomas Svolos: Thank you, Linda, for the reading. Thank you, Florencia, and your transitional remarks there about commentary on the current state of the world are exactly what is going to inform my remarks here today. When I was granted this wonderful opportunity to participate in this meeting, I ended up deciding to do two things. One was to talk about this book in the context of our work as psychoanalysts and our experience of analysis, in our own analysis. That is what I tried to do in my talk last time.

But, given the context for this meeting, what I decided I would like to do today is to put this work to use in trying to say something about civilization today dealing with the pandemic, and I have two things I want to say first to set this up, two quotes from other psychoanalysts. One is short, one is a little longer. The first is from Éric Laurent's paper, "The Real and the Group," where he discusses Lacan's experience in England with Bion and Rickman and so forth. Ah, there it is, published in *The Psychoanalytical Notebooks* and then published again in *The Psychoanalytical Notebooks*.[1] There is this wonderful quote by Laurent towards the end of the text, "Whether it be on a collective scale or for the individual, the psychoanalyst is defined as he who interprets."[2] So, we interpret in our practices, and we have the opportunity to interpret, as he puts it, on the

[1] Éric Laurent, "The Real and the Group," *op. cit.*, pages 59–86.
[2] Éric Laurent, *ibid.*, page 83.

collective scale. This is how we engage with social or political or cultural phenomena, as the person who interprets.

This assertion of Laurent echoes Freud's own opinion about the value of psychoanalysis, and I want to read a paragraph from *The Question of Lay Analysis*, where Freud directly discusses this. He says,

> For we do not consider it at all desirable for psychoanalysis to be swallowed up by medicine [he is talking about therapeutics here] and to find its last resting place in a textbook of psychiatry under the heading "Methods of Treatment," alongside of procedures such as hypnotic suggestion, auto suggestion, and persuasion [or, CBT these days], which, born from our ignorance have to thank the laziness and cowardice of mankind for their short-lived effects. It deserves a better fate, and it may be hoped, will meet with one. As a "depth psychology," a theory of the mental unconscious, it can become indispensable to all the sciences which are concerned with the evolution of human civilization and its major institutions such as art, religion, and the social order. It has already, in my opinion, afforded these sciences considerable help in solving their problems. But these are only small contributions compared with what might be achieved if historians of civilization, psychologists of religion, philologists, and so on would agree themselves to handle the new instrument of research which is at their service. The use of analysis for the treatment of neurosis is only one of its applications: the future will perhaps show that it is not the most important one. In any case, it would be wrong to sacrifice all the other applications to this single one, just because it touches on the circle of medical interests.[3]

So, Freud thought very highly of the work he had developed and believed that it could be put to use for other reasons, such as making sense of civilization or being able to grasp something that is happening in civilization or in art or religion and so forth.

So, I am going to give what I think are seven propositions that I want to make about this pandemic we are going through from the context of Freud and then also Lacan and how they and others since then, Jacques-Alain Miller in particular, have mobilized Freud's way of taking into

[3] Sigmund Freud, "The Question of Lay Analysis," *The Standard Edition of the Complete Psychological Works of Sigmund Freud*, Vol. 20, 1926, London, Hogarth, page 248.

account how libido works within civilization, in introducing a dimension to what we would have to say about society that did not exist before psychoanalysis.

So, let's start with this. In what sense would we say that civilization's response to the pandemic follows the Freudian model? For Freud, the purpose of civilization is to protect the members of civilization, protect against aggression, ensure safety, repress the desires, the libido of the members of civilization for some common good, unite people together—all of these principles that we have been reading about for the last couple of months in *Civilization and Its Discontents*. How has that functioned in our world today? Do we see that anywhere today in the response of global civilization to the pandemic? I would assert that probably the clearest example of that we have seen globally is in New Zealand, which is a very interesting case. In New Zealand, a single leader, Jacinda Ardern, who is a woman—and I will have more to say about that in a second—was able to effectively do that, to take charge in this manner, ensure safety, shut the country down in a way that was more stringent than I believe anything else that I am aware of, except China, and in doing so, essentially at this point, eradicate the virus. People had to stay at home. There were very strict orders put in place, and she proved to be an effective master in this very classical, Freudian sense and got the support of the citizens of New Zealand to do this. In my mind, it is quite remarkable. She had done the same thing several years before. You will recall that there was a mass shooting in Christchurch a couple years ago. It was a racially motivated shooting, and she was able to pull the country together at the same time and pass strict gun control laws, in a country that had significant opposition before that to these laws. She is a rather progressive figure, this prime minister, but in the Christchurch situation, again played the role of Freud's civilization, evoking the importance of safety. One may make different points about the uniqueness of the New Zealand political structure that enables her to do this, but nonetheless, she achieved it. What is interesting to me about this is that she did it in a very unique way. She is a young woman. She had a baby during the course of her term as prime minister. There was a lot of attention given to that and some people were discrediting her ability to lead effectively as a mother, but she led through that, through a very unique utilization of Facebook videos that she would post for the entire country.

It is interesting, when one looks across the globe, at which leaders have been most effective in their countries, in taking charge in this very classical, Freudian way in the name of safety—it has been women. Jacinda Ardern in New Zealand and, in Europe, the example would be Angela Merkel. I think Germany has been very successful as well with regard to the pandemic. And it speaks, perhaps, to a comment from a text that I will draw from later, one where Jacques-Alain Miller comments about the shift of civilization from a civilization based on the masculine logic for all to the feminine logic of the not-all. He comments on the feminization that has occurred in public discourse and how values such as compassion, which are a hallmark of Jacinda Ardern's approach, will now become much more important socially (Merkel, here, is a different matter).[4] So, I think if we are going to take this simple version of Freud's hypothesis around social order and civilization in response to the pandemic, we can see that it applies in this case, it seems to me, fairly clearly. That is Proposition One.

Proposition Two is that it is not always the case. You will note that, for Freud, that part of the fact of the functioning of civilization, the way he describes it, is through the superego, through the leader as the father, the importance of the father for Freud, and through the identification the individual will come to have with the father through love. It is the mechanism of love that is the driving force for this. But Lacan, of course, even very early in his work, pointed out that while in paternal identification, love may have a factor in social organization, that it may not be love that is the most important factor. Lacan drew our attention here to the role of hate in social formations. He identified the importance of hate in the formation of groups. This is a point Lacan made in the 1940s, in the paper on "Logical Time and the Assertion of Anticipated Certainty," where Lacan makes the proposition that I achieve an identification not based on a positive attribution of the thing which I identify with, but rather on the basis of a negative attribution. He says, and this is a quote

[4] Jacques-Alain Miller, "Milanese Intuitions [2]," *Mental Online: International Journal of Mental Health and Applied Psychoanalysis*, #12, May 2003, page 10.

from *Écrits*. He says, "A man knows what not a man is; men recognize themselves among themselves as men; [and] I declare myself to be a man for fear of being convinced by men that I am not a man."[5] It is worth reading, it is a very interesting proposition by Lacan around group formation. Group formation not organized through love, as with Freud, but hate.

And, Éric Laurent has used that passage to say some things about the force of racism today in society.[6] I think we can also see this operative in politics, the success of the current American president in the 2016 elections was a shock to people, but the discourse based on being an American, a great American we can even say, by very clearly defining what is not American, was the logic that propelled the current president to office. It is not a unique thing to the Republicans, because Bernie Sanders, for those who follow American politics, did the exact same thing. He said, "What we are for is not being the 1%." So, we are against the 1 percenters, we are for everyone else in America because the 1 percenters are not part of what this country is about. The campaign built on positive identification, which was the Hilary Clinton campaign, failed.[7] We see this in the pandemic now. In play, at least in the United States, I do not know how this is formulated in Europe, but at least there are many people in the United States for whom the pandemic is a foreign issue. The pandemic was defined by some as an issue on the basis of it being from foreign countries, un-American, a "Chinese infection," and the entire logic of how the country was brought together for some people in responding to the pandemic was as if one is dealing with a foreign threat. So, you can see the role of hatred or negative identification in play. The virus is not something that was affecting us all, and we need to come together to deal with it. Rather, the virus is something from outside, something hated, that we need to respond to. That is my second proposition.

---

[5] Jacques Lacan, "Logical Time and the Assertion of Anticipated Certainty," *Écrits: The First Complete Edition in English*, *Op. cit.*, page 174.

[6] Éric Laurent, "Racism 2.0," published online on the *AMP Blog* on January 29, 2014. Accessed at http://ampblog2006.blogspot.com/2014/01/lq-in-english-racism-20-by-eric-laurent.html on December 27, 2022.

[7] See Chap. 6 of this book for a more extended discussion of this.

Proposition Three: here I do not know the situation in other countries as well as the U.S., but I will say this about the U.S. There are so many people speaking about what is going on and what to do. We have the president. There are some governors that are very prominent—such as Cuomo in New York, Whitmer in Michigan, Hogan in Maryland, and Newsom in California—who have frequent press conferences and are quoted. We have Tony Fauci, who most people probably know is our most prominent medical expert in this area, and Deborah Birx, federal government physician experts. Bill Gates has offered opinions. The economist Jerome Powell, who is the Chair of the Board of the Federal Reserve System, and Steven Mnuchin, the Secretary of the Treasury, have offered their opinions. So, as one follows the discourse about the pandemic, all these figures are speaking and claiming to have authority regarding what to say about our response to the pandemic and how to protect the country. There is an incessant banter back and forth, the incessant buzzing of one person, then the other, then the other. And it occurred to me in thinking about this discord, this lack of a consensus in this country at least, the United States, about how to deal with this, that we are missing a single, universal master here, say, someone along the lines of President Franklin Roosevelt in the era of the Depression and World War II. What I observe now is that we have all these different figures competing to be the master, what Lacan called the S1.[8] We have a swarm of want-to-be S1s, all buzzing with all their talk about this and that and the other, and it is what we might identify as an example of what we refer to in theoretical terminology as a pluralization of the name-of-the-father (another synonym of sorts for S1). There is no name-of-the-father operative right now, no single or universal master, in American discourse and, instead, you have all kinds of figures out there buzzing away trying to take that position. And, indeed, that is my Proposition Three.

What this shows, in fact, is Proposition Four, which is that the place of the S1, the place of the name-of-the-father as a central point in social discourse, at least in the United States, is gone. It cannot be occupied in that sense anymore and, in part, it is that absence, that lack of it that leads to something that got discussed in one of our meetings before, which was the development of a nostalgia for a strong figure to come forward and

[8] Jacques Lacan, *The Seminar of Jacques Lacan: Book XX: Encore (1972–1973)*, *op. cit.*, page 143.

take that. And, in the cases where that does happen, and it has happened not just in the U.S. but in other countries globally, in the cases where that happens, we see that it is never a symbolic father—a universal father of all, a father respectful of the rule of law—that comes to fill this position, but a kind of real father, a *père jouisseur* of sorts, who comes in and is seen by some as strong. It is not a person of a type like Franklin Roosevelt or something like that.[9] This is Proposition Four.

Proposition Five: in all these points, what I am trying to do is take these issues of signification and meaning and authority and libido and show how they get reworked differently and the ways in which our civilization might be like what Freud described and ways in which it is not. So, what else do we see a lot of today? With regard to the pandemic in civilization? It is a turn to experts, to scientists, to public health officials, in the face of a lack of knowledge around what is going to happen. There is a turn by some to knowledge to take the dominant place. As Éric Laurent has commented somewhere, I could not find the reference, if Freud was the one who highlighted the way in which *jouissance* is attached to the S1, it was Lacan who identified the way in which jouissance is linked to S2, to knowledge. It was Lacan's development of the discourse theories in *Seminar XVII*, I think, that highlight this the most, in the discourse of the university where knowledge is in the dominant place, and I think there is a discourse that exists socially with regard to the pandemic that wants that to happen, for our social response to be driven by knowledge.[10] People want the experts to be in the position to give the orders and to structure society. For Lacan, this is something he probably got from Alexandre Kojève, who was very influential in French intellectual life and on Lacan as well, his work on the development of bureaucracy and so forth. I think this discourse is in place now in society and in our response

[9] I develop this more fully in see Thomas Svolos, "Coronavirus and the Hole in the Big Other," *Letters in Quarantine: Psychoanalytic Chronicles of a Pandemic*, Florencia F.C. Shanahan with Marie-Hélène Brousse and Cyrus Saint Amand Poliakoff, editors, New York, Lacanian Press, 2021, pages 443–445. Originally published in *Lacanian Review Online*, March 14, 2020, issue #1 of the *LRO* series "COVID-19." Accessed at https://www.thelacanianreviews.com/coronavirus-and-the-hole-in-the-big-other/ on December 28, 2020.

[10] Jacques Lacan, *The Seminar of Jacques Lacan: Book XVII: The Other Side of Psychoanalysis (1969–1970), op. cit.*

to the pandemic, a desire for a discourse of the university is pushed by many.[11] Allow me to give a very particular vignette about this. I facilitate small group discussions in our medical school at Creighton, and some teachers in a class that I facilitate put together a case, a vignette, for small groups of students to work through. "What would you do if you only have one ventilator, and you have these different kinds of patients come in who need a ventilator to survive? How do you make your decision about who would get the ventilator and who would not?" The intent of the exercise is to help students learn to struggle with difficult decisions you have to make sometimes as a physician. The response of the students is interesting, but one thing that came through with a number of the students was, "Well—can't you just create a formula that will tell us what to do? Give us an algorithm that we can follow, where that algorithm would be the thing driving the decision, one based on research." I think we see this a lot. I assert that this is an example in the way of which we see the discourse of the university operative in society today. This is Proposition Five.

Proposition Six: one very strong strain, at least in the United States, around the pandemic, is we cannot shut things down. Things need to keep moving. We need to get people working. You cannot shut the economy down. The circulation needs to keep going. We need people to work. There is a strong belief among many people that in essence, the circulation of goods, we could say, might even be more important, and to end the circulation of goods may be a worse thing to happen than to have deaths from the pandemic. It is quite obvious, or clear to me at least, that this is a case where we see the discourse of the capitalist in play. Lacan, in addition to the four major discourses that he developed in *Seminar XVII*, also, in a few talks that he gave in Italy in the early 1970s, developed a

[11] See, for example, Éric Laurent, "The Dialogue Lacan-Kojeve on Bureaucracy and on Empire" on the website of the World Association of Psychoanalysis at https://wapol.org/ornicar/articles/lrn0023.htm, accessed on December 27, 2022. Another valuable reference here is Éric Laurent, "Symptom and Discourse," in *Jacques Lacan and the Other Side of Psychoanalysis: Reflections on Seminar XVII*, Justin Clemens and Russell Grigg, editors, Durham, Duke University Press, 2006, pages 229–253.

fifth discourse that he played with for a few years called, "The Discourse of the Capitalist."[12]

Shanahan: It is not a discourse. It is a pseudo-discourse and, maybe later, we can discuss what that means.

Svolos: That would be fine. Note that this is a variation of the discourse of the master, where the positions of the subject and the S1 are inverted, and there is a constant cycling. And, I think it is important to recognize that that discourse or pseudo-discourse has an operative force in the response to the pandemic.

Next proposition, Proposition Seven: in a talk in 2004 that Miller gave in Comandatuba, he talked about how in hearing the cases at that particular Congress of the WAP, that in so many of the cases that were being presented, the cases included people he described as rudderless, without a compass, and disoriented. He introduced a proposition that I think is pretty provocative, which is one in which he states that the discourse of civilization today is no longer structured, as in Freud's time, on the model of the discourse of the master, but closer to the discourse of the analyst.[13] Recall from the exposition that Lacan made about discourse theory the notion that the discourse of the master in essence was the structure of the unconscious in the Freudian moment, and that, in this sense, the discourse of the analyst was the opposite, the flip side or the inverse or the opposite, of the discourse of the master and, as such, analysis could have an operation on the discourse of the master. The hypothesis that we can say is that there is a kind of continuity between the discourse of the unconscious and the discourse of the Other, the discursive world in which people live. So, Miller's point is that in 2004 that the discourse of the unconscious is no longer structured like it used to be on this Freudian model, with the importance of repression, but rather that surplus jouissance, the object *a*, is in the dominant position. It implies that the uncon-

[12] See, for example, Jacques Lacan, "Du discourse psychanalytique: Discours de Jacques Lacan à l'Université de Milan le 12 mai 1972," *Lacan in Italia 1953–1978: En Italie Lacan*, G. Contri, editor, La Salamandra, 1978, pages 32–55. For an elaboration on the Discourse of the Capitalist, see Thomas Svolos, "Introducing the New Symptoms," *Twenty-first Century Psychoanalysis, Op. cit.*, pages 113–126.

[13] Jacques-Alain Miller, "A Fantasy" *Lacanian Praxis: International Quarterly of Applied Psychoanalysis*, #1, 2005, page 15.

scious today is a different unconscious, but it also implies that that is true of the world around us, that if the S1, as I commented earlier, is no longer in the position of mastery, then it is the object *a* that is in the position of what Miller called the "social zenith." I think my impression in thinking about the pandemic is, in a sense, that is the case. The words Miller uses at the beginning of this paper, "rudderless, disoriented, without a compass," these are the words we could use to describe, in the United States at least, the response to the pandemic. In the presentation and discussion about the pandemic and our response, it is first one thing, then the next week, it is another thing, and something else the next week that captivates our attention. There seems to be no clear direction given to what to do. There is a very amusing You Tube video that captures this well—Coronavirus Horse Race—the country moves in one direction, then another, then another: social distancing, flatten the curve, just a little flu, trust the experts, Plaquenil, economic shutdown, Dr. Fauci, and so forth, and in the end, the winning horse is "no one fucking knows."[14] You could compare this to Roosevelt and his leadership of the United States during the Depression and World War II, where they tried things and they would try them and not everything worked, but there was a clear direction that was being taken. There was an ability to unify the country around an S1, a clear direction. We do not see this in the United States at all. Things are very disorganized in the response to the pandemic, with bits of jouissance of one sort or another driving action, and it makes me wonder if indeed that is not a function of what is going on. Miller says, you will recall in this paper, that it is not that the civilization has the structure of the discourse of the analyst, because the connections are not made, the things are not articulated. It just approaches it, or it is like that. And, I think that is another factor, at least in the United States, with what we are seeing now. That is Proposition Seven.

Finally, I want to offer a few remarks that Jacques-Alain made also around that same time, in 2002, in the Milanese Intuitions that I think

[14] Coronavirus Horse Race, accessed at https://www.youtube.com/watch?v=Fn8MxJx_erk on December 26, 2022. For a more serious note on the overall theme of a lack in the Other with regard to the pandemic response, see Thomas Svolos, "Coronavirus and the Hole in the Big Other," *Op. cit.*

very directly address the Freudian text that we are reading.[15] He says, for example, looking at the relationship of politics to the unconscious that if the Freudian proposition is that politics is unconscious, he says, "Yeah, that is fine." And, for Freud, it was all based on this model of identification with the father, repression, and so forth. But Miller is keen to point out that politics is more than that. It is not just this unconscious element. And, as I said earlier, we can see that it is not all about love and positive identification, but negative identification as well, as Lacan introduced. The second hypothesis is that the unconscious is politics in the sense that the unconscious is the discourse of the Other, as I said before. But that discourse may not be structured in the way it was in Freud's moment, and I think our civilization is not that of Freud's, for the most part. The third point he makes is an interesting one, where he says the city does not exist. A certain model of civilization of an imaginary homogenous space along the lines of what they had in ancient Greece is no longer present. Perhaps this is related to the disorientation, a spatial dimension to it. The next point he makes is interesting as well. It is in a section called, "Freud and Queen Victoria," where he says that this repressive model is no longer the case, and he contrasts Queen Victoria with Queen Catherine Millet, who had just written a book, I think, at that moment of his talk. It is called *The Sexual Life of Catherine M.*, in which she documents, and it is an interesting read, in great detail her sexual life.[16] This is not a moment of repression in the Freudian sense. And he talks about the different relationship in Lacan between the signifier and jouissance.

The signifiers killed the drive in Freud, but we see now that the signifiers are a carrier of *jouissance*, we could say, that they carry jouissance in the symbolic, and there is no longer also this classical opposition between pleasure and jouissance, so the propositions in chapter 8 of *Civilization and Its Discontents* about the relationship of the different drives, Eros and aggression and so forth, are not valid for today's society. It doesn't work that way anymore. I do not think this is operative as much as it was

[15] Jacques-Alain Miller, "Milanese Intuitions [1]," *Mental Online: International Journal of Mental Health and Applied Psychoanalysis*, #11, December 2002, pages 9–16; and, Jacques-Alain Miller, "Milanese Intuitions [2]," *Op. cit.*, pages 5–14. This text more recently appeared in *Psychoanalytical Notebooks*, #34, December 2019, pages 81–138.

[16] Catherine Millet, *The Sexual Life of Catherine M.*, New York, Grove, 2002.

before. And then Miller goes on to say that we are in an era of the "not-all." The universal masculine logic of *Seminar XX* defining society is no longer the case, but there are no limits. It is no longer a structure with a limit and an organization and a hierarchy, but we are in a different era with the rise of the feminine, as I indicated before, and both an attack on a culture of masculine virility and a nostalgia to bring that back, a wistful wish for master narratives.

I think we see different configurations socially, country by country, and state by state, around how things are pulled together. You can have, on the one hand, a figure like the President of the United States; on the other hand, you can have somebody like Boris Johnson in England and Macron in France, Merkel in Germany, Jacinda Ardern in New Zealand. Each one of these figures pool different elements, I think, together and create very contingent structures for society.

So, those were my remarks. It is a different kind of reading that I wanted to make. I wanted to open up a space for maybe a different kind of discussion and for comments from different people that would take this work of Freud's, take our approach as psychoanalysts to civilization, and introduce maybe the possibility of saying some different things about the pandemic through our perspective of psychoanalysis, none of which we could have done without Freud. He paved the way for thinking about civilization in this way, and I tried with these propositions to at least open a dialogue on how we might say some things here. Thank you.

Shanahan: Thank you very much, Thomas, and I think it is, as you say, it is a different reading. I am sure that there are elements of the text that people will have questions about and commentaries to make so we are going to introduce a little change in our format today. You are probably already seeing that some others are coming onto your screen. We have decided to invite our commentators and our readers who participated during these eight meetings to be present with us and to contribute to this conversation. Also, we are very much looking forward to what participants may have to say. I invite you to send your questions or commentaries through the Question and Answers box. So, I am delighted to welcome Joanne Conway, Raphael Montague, Gustavo Dessal, Susan McFeely, Neus Carbonell, Roger Litten, Caroline Heanue, Tom Ryan, Linda Clarke, and Sheila Power. We have apologies from Veronique

Voruz, who sent her warmest regards to you all. She could not join us today. We already have a couple of questions in the Question and Answers box so I might start with that, if that is okay, unless there is a pressing remark or comment that anybody would like to make from our panel.

We have some questions in the chat: "I think that Freud still contemporary talks about the superego regarding the modern discourse of the master, the capitalist discourse. He mentions in the last paragraph about how humans have gained control" so I presume it is the last paragraph of the reading of today. Let me go back to it to refresh people. No, I cannot find it. Okay, "Could Thomas comment on this and the economical depression nowadays? In Greece, only the huge businesses remain open. For example, does this have to do with the feminization that Thomas mentioned?" Okay, that is one question. Then, we have another question: "What is implied by using the term discourse?" And a final question: "What do you think about society's reaction to the return to prohibition? For example, the lockdown, a return to the law of the father?" Thomas maybe you want to begin by responding to one or several of these, of your choice?

Svolos: Okay, I would be happy to, but I am also interested in hearing what my fellow panelists have to say about these questions. So, let me take the one about the lockdown, which is interesting because I think the lockdown was implemented in very different ways across the United States. I think part of it could be understood in the classical Freudian sense of the country or the state as the father protecting the citizens through control and forcing abandonment of your wish to travel freely and go to restaurants and whatnot. I think part of it can be understood through this issue of the discourse of the university and the turn to public health experts and putting knowledge in this place where, "Well we have to do it because it is what the experts say to do." So, I think that has a factor in it, but the fact that in the U.S, at least, it was very, very partial, is a function of a kind of competition of these discourses in play. The businesspeople want their businesses to stay open. Some people do not want to make any sacrifices and want to continue to be able to do what they want to do, no sacrifice of my jouissance. And, in the U.S., I do not know if people abroad appreciate that being able to do what I want to do, for some, means showing up at the State Capitol with machine guns and going in the building to protest the lockdown. In the U.S., it is a big deal. And there were people who said, "I am not going to do it. No one is taking this away. This is U.S. This is my freedom. I would rather die than survive." And this type of attachment to a kind of object *a*, in my mind, and a refusal to submit to an S1, is a strong feature of the American response to this. So, in my mind, we can see all these things in play: a very heterogeneous picture depending on where you look.

Gustavo Dessal: Thomas, good morning. Thank you very much for your seven propositions. I found them really interesting. I think they opened many things to figure out, to think, to elaborate. A few days ago, I read, maybe you read it also, a very interesting article entitled, "The Rise of the American Idiot."[17] I found that there is a very interesting connection between what you said about the way the pandemic is being managed in the United States and this article, because I wonder if—given the fact that the legitimate authority no longer exists or maybe, let's rather say, it is in the state of extinction-if this is a new S1, the "idiot" as a new S1, of course I take it as a metaphor of what is happening not only in the United States, of course, but it is globally expanding. The idiot as a new S1, this is the first thing I would like to say, and . . .

Roger Litten: Would that be in the sense of the idiot's jouissance? In the etymological sense? The idiot of jouissance?

Dessal: Yes, maybe. Yes. A good remark, thank you, Roger. Yes. And, concerning what you said about knowledge in the place of the agent, it is interesting because not only in the United States, but in many other countries, society is divided concerning that. Divided in the sense that there are those who trust in knowledge; for example, in all of the sciences, and those who do not, those who mistrust knowledge as something that can take over and give the order. Thank you so much, Thomas, once again.

Svolos: Can I make one response to that? Thank you, Gustavo, I am going to chase that article down. I have not read it yet. I like this idea of the idiot as an S1, although I would say it is an S1 attached to some component of jouissance, as Roger pointed out. It is not an S1 as a pure

[17] Umair Haque, "The Rise of the American Idiot: Why the Rest of the World Doesn't Know Whether to Be Baffled, Horrified, or Dumbstruck by America Right Now," published online at Eudaimonia and Co. Accessed at https://eand.co/the-rise-of-the-american-idiot-dd6c85c445ba on December 27, 2022.

symbolic, but it is rather a kind of, it is an S1 linked with jouissance in some unique way. I think, to your comment about the discourse of the university, what we see is that the discourse of the university generates split subjects. So, in the position of the agent in the discourse of the university, the S2 acts on the object *a* in the position of I think it is called "other" in *Seminar XVII* producing—the lower, right-hand corner of the quadrant in the discourse theory—the split subject. I think that is a function of the discourse of the university is a kind of splitting of the subject that the subjects do not like, as in the effect of bureaucracy. Because it implies some kind of loss or division for the subject in that discourse. In my mind, that is part of what that reaction is. And that reaction is strong in the United States. There is both some belief in science and at the same time some amount of skepticism of expertise on the part of people in the United States—there is a split.

Raphael Montague: Thank you. I think firstly, thanks to Linda for a wonderful reading and thanks very much to Thomas for those seven propositions. What you say about a particular response in certain, let's say, elements of society in the U.S. Those that tend to be heavily armed, let's say, other than the U.S. military, those that tend to be heavily armed—it responds directly to Lacan's proposition with respect to alienation and forced choice, no? It is your freedom or your life. So, as Marie-Hélène Brousse points out in a recent contribution to *Lacan Quotidien*, "The only thing that is guaranteed in this forced choice is a loss."[18] This is what Lacan says in *Seminar XI*. It is interesting to me to refer *Seminar XI* back to your chapter of Freud's *Civilization and Its Discontent*. So, Freud does not speak about unconscious guilt, he speaks about unconscious sense of guilt. It is not at all the same thing. And, I am responding in part to one of the comments here that we had. So, to me, and this is something that Freud repeats. It is almost when he says that it is an unconscious sense of guilt and to me, what we are talking about then is in relation to meaning. It is a sense in terms of the signifying chain and

[18] Marie-Hélène Brousse, "Choix forcé?" *Lacan Quotidien*, #890, May 22, 2020, accessed December 28, 2022, at https://lacanquotidien.fr/blog/wp-content/uploads/2020/05/LQ-890.pdf.

in terms of the subject of the unconscious where the only thing that is guaranteed in alienation in terms of subject construction is this loss. We speak about the forced choice, your freedom or your life. But Freud introduces then a topographical variety of anxiety into his equation, and he is speaking about then a symptom as a substitute for a satisfaction that remains in abeyance, but it is a sexual satisfaction. So, Freud says in terms of the drive train, and this is why *Seminar XI* on the four fundamental concepts is important here. Freud says that it is libidinal elements that turn out to be repressed. Ah, what are these libidinal elements? Well, Lacan would say the only thing that is repressed are signifiers so, you see, libidinal elements are bits of signifiers. Then, we come to separation, which is what we can refer to what is missing in the signifying chain of which the subject is the simple effect, or where is the missing signifier in the locus of the other in terms of the discourse of the unconscious? So, this topographical variety of anxiety, if we read Lacan in *Seminar X*, anxiety is not without an object. Well, what is it that is called up in the signifying chain between S1 and S2 in the void, in the gap, in the signifying chain? Not the vanishing of the subject, but where is the anxiety the subject called up as object, an impossible object. And you see then why for Freud, you run into a problem in terms of analysis interminable because the jouissance, the sense in terms of signifiers that would mean anything that have to be deciphered is S1 linked to S2, which is an indefinite calling up of anxiety in relation to jouissance.

Shanahan: There is something interesting there in one of the questions by a participant as well, how to conceive of guilt and remorse nowadays. I was thinking of what Gustavo was bringing with this idea of the jouissance of, I heard it as the jouissance of the idiot even though Gustavo brings it as an S1, but it is a problem that the S1 has different statuses in Lacan's work and the S1 even though we think about it very quickly as the master signifier, it is not only that but perhaps Thomas or others would like to say something about what Raphael was bringing in terms of the sense of guilt, the unconscious sense of guilt nowadays?

Neus Carbonell: Well, Gustavo Dessal wrote a beautiful text in Spanish, with the title of *Delinquents by Sense of the Solitude*.[19] It is a beautiful article worth translating into English. Dessal argues the two kinds of leaders that we have nowadays. The leaders that are perhaps neurotic and have a certain sense of guilt, and the perverted ones. Today you addressed the same point when talking about contemporary politics. The last paragraph of the chapter today, that I think was added later by Freud at the dawn of the second World War, is worth underlining because of the historical moment in which was added. It is remarkable that Freud talks about the power of destruction of civilization. This pandemic reminds us that the entire planet can be put under the yoke of death. The pandemic reveals that death drive is global: climate change, corruption, individualism.

Shanahan: I am going to give the floor to Joanne. We probably will take two or three questions and comments so raise your hand or write your question, and we will bring then the conversation to a close. Joanne.

Joanne Conway: Thank you, Florencia, and thank you, Thomas and Linda, for today, and I suppose it is a comment I am trying to clarify something, and it echoes a little bit what Neus was saying when she spoke about politics and the rise of the feminine, and you related it to women politicians. My question is in relation to what you were saying about the different forms of leaders that Neus has just mentioned. My question is something around, can politics have any place with the not-all? I mean, is this not in a complete opposition the one to the other, that politics, how does that fit with what you say as far as the rise of the feminine? That was my question.

Svolos: I will just say something very briefly first on the issue of guilt, I would agree. There are probably leaders where guilt is a strong factor, and there are probably some leaders where we do not see a lot of guilt at all. So, absolutely. And, you know, you could do interesting things with that.

[19] Gustavo Dessal, "Los delincuentes por sentimiento de soledad" published on the Zadig Espana site on May 9, 2020, accessed at https://zadigespana.com/2020/05/09/coronavirus-los-delincuentes-por-sentimiento-de-soledad/ on December 26, 2020. Translated into English by Roger Litten and published as "Reclusions" in *Lacanian Review Online*, issue "COVID series" #87 on May 8, 2020. Accessed at https://www.thelacanianreviews.com/reclusions/ on December 26, 2022.

As for Joanne's question, I think the point that I, and this was the point from Jacques-Alain, that I was bringing into my talk—namely the notion that if society is no longer structured under a universal masculine logic, but more under this logic of the not-all, using this *Seminar XX* formulation as a way of saying something about society—he linked that with a decline in the kind of classical notion of masculine virility along with a desire to return to it and find it again.[20] And with a change, I think you could almost say it is a change in the style or the character of discourse in the direction of one that includes things that he described as more classical feminine values like compassion and so forth. So, I would think that it is very possible that, in as much as these terms have utility for us anymore, this sort of masculine/feminine binary, because I think even those, you know, are in flux as well . . . but, I would say that leaders, some leaders in the United States at least, governors, executives, mayors, were being compassionate, were willing to show emotion, were willing to be thoughtful about others, to cry in public—as with Ardern—these kinds of things that 50 years ago would have been seen as inconceivable in a political leader, you see now in political discourse. Ardern was very frank about what she was dealing with as a mother and showed emotion. Showing emotion, in his case crying, sunk the presidential candidacy of Edmund Muskie a half-century ago in the United States.[21] I think that the interesting thing about the Prime Minister of New Zealand, is that you could have those traits—she was very open in talking about her pregnancy and having a young child and talked very openly about that—you can have those traits in a leader who is also very strong. She is strong in the classical sense, in being able to organize society and get things done and have an impact. It unlinks, in my mind, a stereotypical version of masculine/feminine from the notion of being able to occupy a position of S1 and order things, to put it that way.

[20] Jacques-Alain Miller, "Milanese Intuitions [2]," *Op. cit.*, page 10.

[21] Edmund Muskie's alleged episode of crying in defense of his wife and in response to a fabricated attack on him were seen at the time as pivotal factors in his declining stakes in the 1972 Democratic presidential primary, for example. See R. W. Apple Jr., "Edmund S. Muskie, 81, Dies; Maine Senator and a Power on the National Scene," *New York Times*, March 27, 1996, accessed at https://www.nytimes.com/1996/03/27/us/edmund-s-muskie-81-dies-maine-senator-and-a-power-on--the-national-scene.html?searchResultPosition=1, on August 24, 2022, and also https://en.wikipedia.org/wiki/Canuck_letter, accessed on August 24, 2022.

Conway: So, a leader has to be a human being.

Svolos: Well . . .

Montague: Not necessarily.

Conway: Well, you know . . . attempt to be, maybe.

Litten: I just wanted to just make a couple of comments, getting back to what Gustavo said, but just picking up on what Joanne and Thomas and Neus said earlier. About the two modes of leaders, maybe one version would be leaders without guilt, but the one commodity we do not seem to have so much with leaders is shame. Maybe we should not forget, while focusing on this question of guilt, guilty leaders are not necessarily any more useful to us, but we can ask what happened to any leader with a sense of shame. And we see in this chapter something about the relation between guilt and anxiety as topologically related, but we could ask, "What about the role of shame in the modern configuration?" that we hope where we are going with *Seminar XVII* to the question of shame in the last chapter.

Dessal: Absolutely, yes.

Litten: So, then because otherwise we fall into this idea of let's say, character-types of leaders. You have the strong, virile leader, or you have the caring, compassionate, feminine leader, and as both Joanne and Thomas pointed out, the dangers you fall into kind of binary stereotypes of womanly virtues and virile virtues. Whereas, maybe it is more useful to try to place, think about places that can be occupied within the discourse of the all and the not-all including, it is not just which kind of leaders do we get, but which places are available for leaders to occupy within the configuration of current discourses. Which also reminds us that let's say the all and the not-all are not binary exclusive logics. They are logics that are dynamically articulated in exactly the same way that the masculine and the feminine are not separate, it is an articulation between the two, which prevents us from falling into simplistic binaries. In relation to that question of using the mapping of the all and the not-all, I did want to take up what Gustavo has said about the idiot and this idea of the idiot: so jouissance was precisely a comment on the *jouissance* of the idiot because we see otherwise, the idiot just seems, it is a term of insult because we do not agree with these guys because they have low IQ. That is not the point. I think the strong sense of the idiots of jouissance is including, shall we say, because the thing that strikes me about the whole chapter, not just this chapter but the whole thing, is how Freud locates the operator of renunciation as the central articulator between the individual and civilization, and there we can situate what falls under prohibitive culture is all the operators of negation that operate the interface between signifier and jouissance, let's say civilization and the individual whether it is renunciation, sacrifice, castration, prohibition, etc. If we situate the permissive society in contrast to the prohibitive, we see that it is not about the condition in contrast to the prohibitive, it is because the operators of negation no longer function. So, whereas before, it would be the good of all comes above the happiness of the individual, that is the model Freud is working in civilization, it is the Victorian model of prohibition, censorship, renunciation, and castration. Now we have, and it is presumably associated with the new liberal discourse, we have individual right to jouissance, my right to bear arms in the government buildings, and my right to die of the virus if I wish to and endanger everybody else because my individual right to jouissance is unchallenged, and it is not clear what the operator is that can challenge my individual right to jouissance, which has, let's say, been supported by three centuries of the neoliberal discourse. So, whereas before, civilization depends on the individual renunciation of happiness in order to reclaim it in the guise of the old, now suddenly we have the individual idiots of jouissance, but the question of how those rights are going to be articulated in the frame of some greater good that would be a viable civilization certainly becomes a question that we have not solved.

Shanahan: We haven't yet, and we won't today and probably . . .

Litten: And it is interesting how the pandemic then forces that question to the fore because the pandemic is not something that can be solved in terms of individual rights to *j*ouissance nor the individual right to . . . It is something that requires a collective solution, but we do not have collective operators that might actually allow us to address those questions.

Susan McFeely: Really, my comment, I have to say, I am just conscious we are coming close to time. My comment is really more about this invention of *Civilization and Its Discontents* and in the particular time that we have all found ourselves in, as Neus has spoken of very much that you compare the times but, in particular, where each one of us have been confronted with our own relationship to solitude, and I suppose I wanted to thank you, Florencia, of course, for this invention because it has, in a sense, supported all of us to remain awake, to not cover, and to confront and to step out of our solitude at times. My second comment is about a reader. It was an interesting invention for us to think of reading out loud and for me, it was one of the most fantastic experiences, and I wanted to thank you for that and in fact, it really made me think very long and hard about, in fact, the solitude of reading silently sometimes, so thank you so much for that.

Shanahan: Thank you, Susan, as well, and everyone who participated in this reading seminar. The first one, when we started, I personally did not even know what Zoom was. I had to go to Google and find out what this platform was, how it worked. This could not have been possible without Linda Clarke who has given many, many hours, but also who did a beautiful reading today, which is a great way to conclude this initiative, this adventure. We have met a lot of new people along the way, and I am delighted for that. We have connected with part of the world where I did not even know psychoanalysis was in existence in such a lively way, and I think we can take this as the beginning of what the contingency has allowed us to encounter. We go back to Neus' first commentaries in terms of the price to be paid, the loss to be admitted, and the gain because that is what the loss makes possible. So, I thank you very much for being there. These meetings will be published in the form of the recording videos online on the ICLO website but everyone who paid with their presence, with their bodies, with their voice, with their words in the commentaries, in the questions and answers, will know that that gives something extra, so thank you very much. See you again. Bye.

Part IV

The Horizon of Subjectivity of Our Time

The following section derives from a series of encounters—residues of an encounter with some social, political, or historical event of the moment that invited commentary. Jacques Lacan tasked psychoanalysts with taking stock of what is happening in the world around them:

> Of all the undertakings that have been proposed in this century, the psychoanalyst's is perhaps the loftiest, because it mediates in our time between the care-ridden man and the subject of absolute knowledge. This is also why it requires a long subjective ascesis, indeed one that never ends, since the end of training analysis itself is not separable from the subject's engagement in his practice.
>
> Let whoever cannot meet at its horizon the subjectivity of his time give it up then. For how could he who knows nothing of the dialectic that engages him in a symbolic movement with so many lives possibly make his being the axis of those lives? Let him be well acquainted with the whorl into which his era draws him in the ongoing enterprise of Babel, and let him be aware of his function as an interpreter in the strife of languages. As

for the darkness of the mundus around which the immense tower is coiled, let him leave to mystical vision the task of seeing the putrescent serpent of life rise up there on an everlasting rod.[1]

These different texts, mostly short, are my attempt to take stock of the world outside the psychoanalytic office.

[1] Jacques Lacan, "The Function and Field of Speech and Language in Psychoanalysis," *Écrits: The First Complete Edition in English, op. cit.*, page 264.

5

Psychoanalysis

Abstract Psychoanalysis itself—the practice of psychoanalysis and the institutions of psychoanalysis—should also be interpreted, which is the basis for the three papers included in this chapter. When the COVID pandemic developed, the growing practice of psychoanalysis through technology—by video or phone—became much more common and put the status of the body in the virtual psychoanalytic experience in question. In as much as Jacques Lacan defines psychoanalysis as the "encounter of the bodies," a proposition of the encounter with the imaginary body and the real body itself is advanced, drawing on the experience of the analyst and analysand. A second paper in this chapter presents a historical sketch of the analytic act based on its own articulation with historical changes in civilization itself. In the final paper in the chapter, a theoretical approach to psychoanalytic institutions—to the School itself, in the Lacanian orientation—defines a distinction between the imaginary functioning of psychoanalytic institutions, itself based on Jacques Lacan's use of the notion of "empire," and the place of desire in the function of the institution.

Keywords Psychoanalytic concept of the body • Virtual psychoanalysis • Analytic act • History of Psychoanalysis • School of Psychoanalysis • Imaginary dimension of group • Empire

T. Svolos, *Culture and Politics on the Couch*, The Palgrave Lacan Series,
https://doi.org/10.1007/978-3-031-61365-4_5

The first text below was an invited lecture delivered May 23, 2021, at the 19th International Congress of the New Lacanian School, on the theme of "Bodily Effects of Language." One of the themes of the Congress was "Bodies in Lockdown," and the practice of virtual psychoanalysis by phone and video was one of the issues most addressed in the context of the theme. While the "encounter of the bodies" is frequently cited to highlight the impossibility or difficulty of virtual psychoanalysis, I attempted to take account of my experience as a psychoanalyst and as an analysand of virtual analysis with a theory of the body derived from Lacan's notion of the libidinal object.

The following text was a response to an invitation from Brazilian colleagues, who were working on "The Analytic Act and Civilization," for their Study Days. I was asked to contribute a preparatory text on the theme prior to the meeting. The very historical approach to the analytic act within the history of psychoanalysis provided the context for this text in which I attempt to develop a historical schema of the analytic act.

The final text is the Opening Lecture that I delivered on February 10, 2023, for the 15th Clinical Study Days of Lacanian Compass on the theme "The Empire of Images." The Council of Lacanian Compass requested a talk about psychoanalytic groups and Schools in the context of that theme. Drawing on Lacan's notion of Empire from Seminar XVI, *I observed that psychoanalytic institutions, as true of many institutions, are empires—empires of images, to engage the precise formulation of Lacan. But, in addition to the imaginary dimension of all groups, in the WAP and its institutions, I argue that the School is organized to also support desire, the desire for psychoanalysis, and what Lacan called the Freudian Cause.*

5.1 The Body in the Virtual Psychoanalytic Experience

Alexander Stevens asked me to make a few remarks about psychoanalysis conducted using the technology of the telephone or video during the time of the pandemic. I want to preface what I will say with a remark about the place from which I speak: not only from the perspective of the analyst, but also from my experience as an analysand. The work I did with my first analyst was largely over the phone. As for my second analyst: I saw him for what we call the *tranches*, those condensed periods of a week in another city with many sessions, but also for some time on a weekly basis by video.

I want start with a reference to the classical phase of Lacan's teaching, the transference described as a function of the subject supposed to know. Many people come seeking analysis with a type of transference in place. If we go back to Freud's formulation of transference as transference love, we might call this transference of the analysand, prior to the encounter with the analyst, a transference "infatuation." It can be an imaginary transference that is in place prior to the first session: some image in the future analysand's mind of what might happen in psychoanalysis or image of what knowledge will come out of the encounter with the psychoanalyst. In some cases, this is based on what the patient has heard about the analyst, or from hearing and watching the analyst speak, or reading their works. I think that a task of the analyst in those first sessions is to somehow grasp something of the real or the symptom at stake for the analysand. That act of the analyst in grasping that, in the analyst's interpretation, functions to set the treatment in motion, piercing the imaginary suppositions of the analysand about why they were there, what the analysand wanted, with a reading of the words of the analysand that is other than what the analysand expected. The effect of this is, according to Lacan in *Seminar XIX*, based on encounter of the bodies (the body of the analysand and that of the analyst) in the preliminary sessions, an encounter that leads to a shift into the analytic discourse.[1] In thus bringing up the issue of the bodies, we might then reframe the analytic experience from the vantage point of the object, of the analyst in the place of the Other having the object *a* for the analysand as a subject. But, I believe, we must recall that this object *a* is the object of the subject given by or extracted from the subject and placed on or in the Other. What is important here is not always the Other's body, the analyst's body, let's say, as such, but the use the analysand makes of the Other as having the object *a*. The most

[1] Jacques Lacan, *The Seminar of Jacques Lacan: Book XIX: . . . or Worse (1971–1972)*, Cambridge, Polity, 2018, page 204.

concrete formulation of this by Lacan was in Chapter 17 of *Seminar X*.[2] This is the striking description by Lacan of the fact that the oral object is not the breast of the mother, as is typically described, but rather the mamma, which was originally that portion of the embryo that in the developing fetus is extruded from, separated from, the future human being and is the first object of nourishment. The subject takes a piece of itself, embryologically, as its first object, which is then transferred to the placenta that parasitizes the mother for the nourishment of the developing fetus and then transferred to the nipple on the breast. For Lacan, the object is cut from and by the subject and placed on the Other.

These objects of the body can end up in what Jacques-Alain Miller refers to as their natural forms, on the body, as pieces or scraps of a fragmented body associated with a cut and a rim, such as, for the oral object, the nipple on the breast. However, the world we live in today has expanded the range of places where that object may be placed beyond that of its natural forms, in the body. The place of the Other has expanded dramatically, most notably with the creation of the internet and the whole virtual world. This is certainly what Lacan was hinting at in *Seminar XVII*, when he developed his notion of the *lathouse*.[3] In 2008, we developed this substantially for the WAP Congress in our work together on the objects *a* in the psychoanalytic experience. Recall Jacques-Alain Miller's argument for the Congress, in which he showed how each one of the classical objects (oral, anal, phallic, scopic, invocatory) might be extended or transferred beyond their bodily or natural form to objects of culture and objects of sublimation.[4] As for the oral object, as an example, this would be nothing more, in a logical sense, than an extension of the original cut of the object from the subject in its embryonic state to the placenta then to the mother's breast and now to a different Other. We should keep in mind that this is, of course, a historical phenomenon, this shift in the Other to include the virtual Other and expansion in the range of possibilities of places for

---

[2] Jacques Lacan, *The Seminar of Jacques Lacan: Book X: Anxiety (1962–1963)*, Cambridge, Polity, 2014, pages 230–242.

[3] Jacques Lacan, *The Seminar of Jacques Lacan: Book XVII: The Other Side of Psychoanalysis (1969–1970)*, *op. cit.*, page 162.

[4] Jacques-Alain Miller, "AMP 2008: The Object *a* in the Analytic Experience," *Lacanian Compass*, #1:9, January 5, 2007, pages 4–9.

the object. This is something that has happened very recently in human history.

So, with this account in place, responding to Alexandre's question, I would propose the following. First, as with so much of what we do, there are no general rules. I don't think we have a rule for analysis over the phone or by video. Rather, we must take into account the situation of each analysand one by one. Can a transference be established, in the sense I described above, in an analysis conducted by technology? Might the analytic discourse as developed in an analysis conducted by technology put the subject in place in its relationship with the object *a* held in the Other, the virtual Other? I believe the answer to both of these questions is "yes," it is possible, and I suggest that I have experienced this in the place of the analysand and in the place of the analyst.

That said, I will offer a few additional observations. The first is that there are situations where I believe it is not possible. Certain subjects, for one reason or another, do not want to or struggle with the ability to have an analytic experience using technology. A general observation is that the more comfortable a person is with the world of technology, the more likely that they might take to analysis using technology. The age of the analysand—as this new Other has come into being in the less than the time of a human life—can be a factor here, but that is certainly not the only one, as there are plenty of older people who have become quite comfortable with technology and *vice versa*. Indeed, if a subject's Other can incorporate a virtual Other, then I believe analysis by technology is possible, even if not preferable.

5.2 History and the Link of the Analytic Act with Civilization

The axis of work of the Tenth Study Days of the Escola Brasileira de Psicanálise on "The Analytic Act and Civilization" at once raises the question about the relationship of our work as analysts with the civilization in which we work.[5] Lacan, of course, made use of topology for a unique way to approach the relationship of civilization with the unconscious. Unlike Freud's model of a bag, with an inside and an outside, as a model for the speaking being in the world, for Lacan, there is a special relationship of the subject with their civilization that he figures with the mobius strip and the Klein bottle. This is a very different figuration of the interior and exterior, in which we recognize that that which is most intimate for the speaking being might be perceived as from the outside, or *vice versa*, this notion of *éxtimacy*, connecting the speaking being and civilization without the strict boundary of Freud.

We might ask the question of the relationship of the analytic act with civilization on this basis. And, to that end, I would like to propose that we might look at aspects or dimensions of the analytic act in an historical manner and query their very relationship to civilization, not civilization as a monolithic and enduring entity, but civilization as an historical phenomenon.

Thus, we might start with the first and basic Freudian analytic act of interpretation—in which the analyst provides meaning, which is extracted from the analysand's unconscious in the analytic experience, to an unconscious formation of an analysand. There is, at least, an echo of this in Lacan's rereading of this at the earliest moment of his work, using linguistics. The symbolic dominates the imaginary, and the symbolic itself is ruled over by the name-of-the-father. For the purposes of this little paper, I will characterize this as a first dimension of the analytic act and assert that it is linked to a moment of civilization in which the name-of-the-father dominates.

We might characterize a second dimension of the analytic act as the way in which the analytic act introduces equivocation in all of its forms. This second dimension of the analytic act follows the first and correlates, we might say, with a moment of civilization in which the name-of-the-father is plural. The universalism of the first moment has been broken, and new structures of meaning are introduced. Phonemes in civilization

[5] This text originally appeared in Portuguese as "História e a conexão do ato analítico com a civilização" in *Boletim Travessias* [electronic journal of the Escola Brasileira de Psicanálise] #5. Accessed October 27, 2021, at https://ebp.org.br/sp/historia-e-a-conexao-do-ato-analitico-com-a-civilizacao/.

itself take on a different value. In literature, this is the moment of modernism.

A third dimension of the analytic act is what I will designate its senseless character. This is the analytic act without meaning, or an interpretation or act disconnected from meaning. This is an interpretation of the analyst that does not have symbolic value or some other act of the analyst that is not a verbal interpretation as such. Sometimes, we hear and read in testimonies of the pass about the effects of the analyst's bodily acts on the analytic experience of the analysand: perhaps, a look from the analyst; some grunt or other noise from the analyst; or, the analyst slapping a hand on the table. All of these acts are, I assert, disconnected from the symbolic, but have their force or their impact through their ability to catch hold of the real in some way or another. This characterizes yet another historical moment in our civilization, that moment in which, as Jacques-Alain Miller put it in "A Fantasy," the object *a*, that bit of the real, is in the dominant place in society.[6] The analytic act is no longer interpretation related to meaning, but something else. We can recall here all the conversations about the post-interpretive era or post-Oedipal interpretation. That dimension of the analytic act, which grasps a bit of the real, comes into psychoanalysis at this moment of civilization. Our act, in this moment that many name postmodernity or hypermodernity, correlates with this historical structure of civilization.

Indeed, this is the very argument that Miller makes in this paper from 2004, namely if the discourse of the analyst is the other side of the discourse of civilization, which has for long been the discourse of the master, secured by the name-of-the-father, what about today, where civilization is no longer structured according to the discourse of the master, but the discourse of the analyst? Miller makes one subtle, but I think important, point about this. He states that in civilization's discourse today, while the elements may be structured like the discourse of the analyst, with the object *a* in the position of the agent, the elements themselves are disconnected. Thus, it is not a true discourse, but rather a fragmented discourse, a kind of pseudo-discourse. The act of the analyst in connecting the elements into a true discourse is characteristic of what I will term a fourth

[6] Jacques-Alain Miller, "A Fantasy," *Op. cit.*

aspect of the analytic act, the interpretation in its *sinthomatic* dimension, the way in which an interpretation might resonate in the registers of the imaginary, the symbolic, and the real. I gave an example of this from my own analysis in a seminar I gave in Miami, published in a book as *The Aims of Analysis: Miami Seminar on the Late Lacan*. An interpretation from my analyst had multiple reverberations in the imaginary, the symbolic, and the real dimension of my lived experience—connecting to an image of my body, a kind of symbolic mandate, and bits of the real that were repeating themselves in my mind. Furthermore, it was immediately after this interpretation that I was able to see for the first time, as a kind of veil was lifted (itself, another link to the interpretation), my object *a*, the semblant of being that I cherished that had been driving my life and about which, before, I was completely blind. It was the most transformative moment of my experience of analysis, whose impact, I assert, was a function of it connecting elements, like a *sinthome*, a dimension of the analytic act for today's civilization.

5.3 The Empire of Images and the Counterbalance of Desire

Thomas Svolos: I want to first thank the Council of the Lacanian Compass for the invitation to serve as the Chair of the Scientific Committee this weekend. It's a real joy and one of the wonderful jobs in the Compass.

Now, what is the logic behind our work at a Study Days? It struck me as we were developing the program that this follows the logic that Lacan articulates in his paper on logical time.[7] The argument is the "instant of the glance." The Scientific Director is asked, once the title is made, to construct a first glance at the theme, with an argument, to lay some coordinates down for the work ahead. It is done quickly, in a flash, at the time of initial planning.

And then for months, leading up to this event, the Clinical Study Days, through our video conferences and meetings, we're working on the

[7] Jacques Lacan, "Logical Time and the Assertion of Anticipated Certainty," *Écrits: The First Complete Edition in English*, *Op. cit.*, pages 161–175.

theme in a "time for comprehension." And, most importantly, a group of members and colleagues identify cases that they believe will shed some light on the theme. The main job of the Scientific Committee is to pick those cases that do that best and work with the presenters sometimes to refine the presentations.

Finally, each one of us will leave here, perhaps, with a "moment to conclude." Azeen Khan will share hers in her coda—a moment to conclude at the end of the meeting. So, I suggest that as a way of thinking about the logic of our work in the Study Days.

So, I was asked to be the Scientific Director and I thought that, other than lots of organization and logistics, my work was done when I completed the argument, but I was wrong. The Council informed me that I have to speak about something on the theme of the Empire of Images and, furthermore, I was asked to speak about the Lacanian Compass and the institutional state of our group around this theme of Empire of Images. And I said, well, this is a challenge. How am I going to talk about the Lacanian Compass in the context of the Empire of Images? It was not obvious to me for a long time.

I'll start with this remark. I'm going to say something that I recall speaking about a little bit at my last stint in this job, which was in 2017, at the Clinical Study Days in Miami. I don't remember the theme, but, in any case, we had a Study Days in Miami. And it was a momentous moment, because at the end of 2016, the Compass became a formal legal group in the United States. We became an incorporated, non-profit organization, and we did that a couple months before the Study Days. And, it was around then also that we became a formal group of the New Lacanian School.

So, I remember reflecting on that in my remarks in 2017 and taking a look at the history of the Compass, which some of the people here know all about and participated in from the beginning. But, some of you are new. In any case, I wanted then and want again today to highlight a point about the word "image," one of the words in "Empire of Images," in the sense of imaginary.

When we started the Compass, we didn't have an imaginary. We just had an event, the Clinical Study Days. It was held first in New York in 2005. We just called it Clinical Study Days. Alicia Arenas, Maria Cristina

Aguirre, and I put together that first program and there were three cases presented and discussed by Vicente Palomera on, if I recall the theme, the real or the body.

And then, we decided to do another, and again every year after that. But we weren't a group. We didn't have members. There was no imaginary consistency to what we were doing. There was no inside and no outside of the Compass. It was just the three of us organizing this event. I thought maybe we could at least get a signifier. Maybe we could get a signifier, and I proposed Lacanian Orientation in the United States, and it was rejected by the president of the World Association of Psychoanalysis at the time who said, "no."

We were told "You can say this is sponsored by some members of the World Association of Psychoanalysis in the United States." So, we didn't have a name, a signifier. All we could say is we members of the WAP were sponsoring this event. So, for years, we worked with no imaginary consistency, no signifier, no membership, no inside, no outside. We just kept doing things because that was our desire.

Sometime around 2010, we did get a signifier. It was given, I believe, by Jacques-Alain Miller in conversation with some of us, I don't know the details as I was not there. He said, "why don't you take the name of your journal, *Lacanian Compass*, as a signifier for the group?" So, in 2010, we had a signifier, but still no imaginary (no membership, no consistency).

We didn't have to deal with imaginary things, like members. Then in 2016, we had a group and were named a group of the School. We had members, people applied, we had a process, who's in, who's out, and I remember asking six years ago at the Clinical Study Days, how are we going to deal with this imaginary?

I asked if this was going to cause us some problems and discontent, as can occur with all the imaginary phenomena that come with the existence of groups—phenomena of love, hate, rivalry, and jealousy and so forth. I'll offer my thoughts about where we've gotten as the Compass with regard to this signifier "image."

But, first, what about this other signifier in the theme, "empire"? It's a powerful word. Of course, it evokes the ancient empires with hierarchy and power and order (in contrast to the disorder attributed to some others, rightly or wrongly, globally at that time). It has some more contemporary resonances, for those of you who study philosophy and things like that, with a book published 30 years ago by Michael Hardt and Antonio Negri, titled *Empire.*[8] Negri and Hardt looked at contemporary society from the perspective of empire. You may not know the book, but probably a lot of people in the room remember that Jacques-Alain Miller commented on their book *Empire* in the Milanese Intuitions 20 years ago or so, in a discussion as well about institutional matters (it was, I believe, related to the formation of the Italian school).[9]

But this word "empire" bothered me. What sense can I make of it regarding images and regarding the institution Lacanian Compass? What am I going to say about the Compass as an empire? It wasn't obvious. And then, I recalled a reference that Lacan makes to the word, the signifier, "empire." It's in *Seminar XVI*, one of my favorite chapters in the seminar. It's called "Knowledge and Power." It's been published formally in French.[10] We don't have an approved translation, yet, in English. What does Lacan say about empire? He says the following: We are forced to conceive of the imaginary because of the *Umwelt*, which is a German word that means outer world, environment. He adopted it from Jakob von Uexküll, who was ahead of his time: he was a type of biologist and ecologist who was very interested in the relationship within the natural world between organisms and their environment.

Parenthetically, I will note I read one of his books, it's published in English, it's been translated, he was roughly a contemporary of Lacan.[11] And Lacan was keen on von Uexküll, he discusses him in *Seminar XI*, in *Seminar XVI*, and I think in *Television*, there's one reference to von Uexküll.

Lacan notes that we have to, as organisms, take things in for their conservation, this defines the relationship between the organism and the *Umwelt*.

[8] Michael Hardt and Antonio Negri, *Empire*, Cambridge, Harvard University Press, 2001.

[9] Jacques-Alain Miller, "Milanese Intuitions [1]," *Mental Online: International Journal of Mental Health and Applied Psychoanalysis*, #11, *ibid.*

[10] Jacques Lacan, "Savoir Pouvoir," Chapter 19 in *Le séminaire Livre XVI: D'un Autre à l'autre*, Paris, Seuil, 2006, pages 295–307.

[11] See Jakob von Uexküll, *A Foray into the Worlds of Animals and Humans: with A Theory of Meaning*, Minneapolis, University of Minnesota Press, 2010.

Well, if we consider Lacanian Compass as an organism, taking things in from the *Umwelt* is the question of membership. Who is taken in, and who is out? This is an imaginary construction. Going back to the reference in *Seminar XVI*: in this passage of the Seminar, Lacan has an interesting etymological reverie, like he does from time to time, and he links "empire" with "emporium," and says they're drawn from the same Latin root.

They're the same thing—for both, according to Lacan, it's about ordering, which is part of the traditional role of the master: to give orders, but also counting. Considering an institution such as a group or a School as an empire highlights this function similar to an emporium—there is an act of ordering and of counting. For us in the Compass and the NLS, it's one of the essential judgments we make in the forming a school or a group.

Who is in? Who is out? How do we order it? What are the processes? In the New Lacanian School, there are practicing analysts, analyst members of the school, and analysts of the school, societies; and, as for groups, there are groups, affiliated groups, associated groups, and initiatives.

So, all this ordering that goes on. We create, in creating our groups and schools, empires of images. This is very consistent with Lacan's reading, as Lacan says what is ordered and what is counted <u>is</u> the imaginary. It is imaginary. It is an ordering of the *Umwelt*, which is precisely what we do as the Compass or the School. The Compass and the School are, in fact, empires of images, as Lacan defines it in *Seminar XVI*.

Now, there is an interesting sidebar to this: Lacan continues in the *Seminar*, and he says this is all based on a particular belief that has been accepted for a long time: a belief that power and knowledge are the same thing. Lacan says that is a fact of the ancient world—this belief, this fantasy, that power and knowledge are the same. Think of the philosopher king of Plato, for example.

Was it ever true? I don't know. Is it true now? Absolutely not. If we learn nothing from the pandemic, it's that knowledge and power do not have a very close relationship with one another, as we observe the social response across the globe to the pandemic.

This observation of Lacan regarding a belief held that knowledge and power are the same thing strikes me as not without a relationship to a comment he makes in *Seminar XX*. You'll recall he says that pre-modern forms of knowledge are all notable for the fantasy of the inscription of the sexual bond, which, for Lacan, does not exist. And the difference between modern and pre-modern is an important point of periodization for Lacan. So, if we take this idea of the empire of images, how do we make sense of this empire, thinking of knowledge and power in our work in the WAP?

Regarding psychoanalysis, I think Lacan recognized the failure of the empire of images in the IPA's approach to psychoanalytic organizations. There are many ways that we can conceptualize the failure of the empire Freud built, but one of them is that the founders of the IPA stuck to the ancient notion of knowledge equaling power. Those who held the power in the organization of the IPA were presumed to have knowledge about psychoanalysis and *vice versa*—this is the hold that the training and supervising analysts have over the institutions in the IPA.

Lacan's practice and his teaching broke that up, and he was exiled for it. And he talks about being exiled in this chapter of *Seminar XVI*, re-ordered in the empire.

In his next seminar, *Seminar XVII*, you'll recall, Lacan takes the separation of knowledge and power a step further—I argue that he makes them separate discourses. The discourse of the master is the discourse of power, the master giving orders is in the position of the agent. And the discourse of the university is the discourse with knowledge in the position of the agent. And they're separate discourses, along with the separation of the discourses of the analyst and the hysteric.

One of Lacan's other ways out of this empire, for a psychoanalytic organization, was the development of the Pass. The Analysts of the School are not necessarily in positions of power. They don't run the schools, but we all suppose they are in positions of knowledge. We all await to hear and read the testimonies of the Analysts of the School, for what new knowledge they bring to our work as psychoanalysts. And that's what going through the Pass is all about. The knowledge developed in psychoanalysis is largely through that. But, separate from that, the power resides in the school. It struck me that that is an interesting institutional way of separating knowledge and power. This is unlike the IPA, where the training analysts are assumed to have both power and knowledge and run the schools in the IPA.

What about the Compass? How have we managed in our work to mitigate the effects of the imaginary since 2016, now that we have an imaginary construction? I would say that the Compass and the School are not only empires of images. This is in part because of the work of the Pass, but there are other institutional practices as well that counterbalance the empire of images and the conflation of knowledge and power.

What about membership? In the IPA, membership is based on the accomplishment of these imaginary things—take a certain curriculum of classes, have so many sessions of supervision, with so many different supervisors on so many cases, and be in analysis for so many sessions. If a person accomplishes these things, they can become a member of certain groups in the IPA.

In the WAP, however, to become a member of a School, it's all about your desire. It's all your desire. So yes, there's the empire, the imaginary phenomena (analysis, supervision, cartels, etc.), but the empire is built upon desire. Desire is the counterbalance, in my view, to the empire of images.

It's an interesting way of explaining what I now refer to, my apologies to my friend, as the Arango principle. Juan-Felipe Arango has given us a principle in how to think about membership. He says a person should be made a member of a group or a member of the School when everybody assumes that they're a member of the group or a member of the School already. The person has to request it, of course, but if the general sense is that the person is acting like a member of the group or School with decided desire, then it is probably time to make the person a member.

I'll tell you about a little parapraxis of mine this week regarding this principle. I was writing up short draft biographies for the presenters for the program, and I said, in my description of Anna De Filippi, that "Anna De Filippi is a member of Lacanian Compass practicing in Houston." Anna replied to me in an email, "Well, Tom, I'm actually not a member of the Lacanian Compass."

Audience: Laughter.

Svolos: So, treat that, Anna, as a sign that your desire, your engagement with the work, comes through as that of a member, even though you haven't gotten the imaginary designator yet of a member. We do have an imaginary, but it's not only an imaginary. It is built upon a desire.

Let us also take a look at how the Compass manages its Clinical Study Days. We in the Council have the power regarding the Study Days. But we don't put ourselves in the position of knowledge. [*Sotto voce*] Of course, I'm saying that while I'm standing here at the podium talking.

Audience: Laughter.

Svolos: But, the heart of the Study Days is to give the floor to new people, to young members, to people who are not members of the Compass, to share and present their cases.

They have knowledge. We want to learn from it. We've structured the entire event around the knowledge that people extract from their work and for the most part, they're not necessarily people who have a lot of power in running the Compass right now. That's a very intentional choice we've always made within the Compass. We give people the chance to present because they have knowledge. They have have extracted some knowledge in the cases they present that leads us to think they have something to say about the theme.

The imaginary gives consistency, as Lacan develops in his unpublished *Seminar XXII, RSI*.[12] That's one of the features of the imaginary. Another institutional practice we are developing is to break up the consistency with permutations, so that different people are in different positions within the Compass. The consistency of the image is not what it's all about.

Now, nonetheless, people complain about the Compass sometimes, the NLS, the WAP. And what's interesting about the complaints about our psychoanalytic groups is that it's often about some imaginary dimension of them. That's been my observation, complaints that sometimes miss the issue of the desire at stake.

I would suggest if there is a symbolic dimension to what we do, it is what Lacan called the Freudian cause. It's like a symbolic mandate to advance psychoanalysis. At the same time as we have this imaginary and this symbolic, we also always try to identify that opaque real that is animating the group and the school, which is a subject. There's some real

[12] Jacques Lacan, *The Seminar of Jacques Lacan: Book XXII: RSI (1974–1975)*, unpublished.

there, too. But, to take the Council and our work as an example: sorting out what really is imaginary, with all of its deceptions and so forth, from desire, from the symbolic and the real, is not always easy in making decisions.

The politics of the decisions are very difficult sometimes. I am certain we've made mistakes in sorting that out, probably largely mistakes in leaning too much on the imaginary. It is inevitable. But, it is probably equally true that some of the decisions made by the Council, which are decisions we try to make to foster the desire of psychoanalysis, get interpreted through an imaginary lens of hate or envy or aggression and so forth.

Deception goes many ways when it comes to the imaginary. That too is part of the phenomenon of working in a School. But our task, in the Council, and as members of the Compass and as members of a School, is to try to knot the empire of images as much as we can to desire, the desire for psychoanalysis.

We strive to knot this imaginary empire to desire and to our symbolic mandate to provide a Compass, weathering the encumbrance of the imaginary consistency that we now have in Lacanian Compass, and trying to keep our focus on the symbolic mandate and the opaque real that is at the heart of our desire as a School.

But it's never a done deal. And must always be reinterpreted. Always, always. As the school is a subject, and like a subject in analysis, there is interminable work in keeping desire alive.

6

American Partisan Politics

Abstract In the United States, the 2016 presidential elections were a surprise to many observers and political pundits. Voting and political affiliation had previously been constructed on a model of positive identification, on the alignment of voters with politicians with whom they felt a positive identification. The 2016 election highlighted, rather, the importance of negative identification of the voters. Voters with perhaps little personal identification with candidates chose candidates on the basis of shared objects of hatred, of negative identification. This hatred is linked to a certain disgust with some aspect of the Other that the voter wishes to avoid. This was true in the election of nominees and elected officials from both major parties. A second text in the chapter explores one path for politics that subverts the force of identification.

Keywords Political affiliation • Positive versus negative identification • 2016 Presidential election • Hate and fear in politics • Return Day • Bury the Hatchet

The results of the 2016 presidential elections in the United States were a surprise to many (the unconscious is all about surprise), and they provided the occasion for the following two texts. The first text has a focus on identity in its political dimension and the ways in which identity today is articulated with

T. Svolos, *Culture and Politics on the Couch*, The Palgrave Lacan Series,
https://doi.org/10.1007/978-3-031-61365-4_6

group formation linked to hatred, or the aggressive libido. The second text articulates a path, a psychoanalytic path, for the subversion of identity and all the problems linked to identity-based group formation.

6.1 The Unconscious in Play in Voting Today

Many have commented on the shock of this election. And, many are asking themselves now—how could this have happened?

Psychoanalysis has its own contribution to this political analysis.

Let us look at voting as, for example, the formation of a group, a statement of the way in which one affiliates with a group, or the way in which people assimilate into a group.

The Clinton campaign based its strategy on a series of positive identifications. The Democratic party is pro-union, pro-African American, pro-Latino, pro-LGBTQ, pro-women, and so forth. In that way, the party situated itself as a series or a group of positive points of identification. And, indeed, identification was, for psychoanalysis and for Freud, in Group *Psychology and the Analysis of the Ego*, itself the logic of group formation. One group, however, did not see its representation in that group of identities gathered together under the Democratic campaign, namely the white, blue-collar families of the upper Midwest who have seen such economic devastation (loss of manufacturing jobs) with the rise of global capitalism over the past 30 years—a group whose departure from the Democratic party to vote Republican was decisive.

And what about the Trump campaign? This campaign formed itself on the basis of an identification as "American," yet not on a series of positive identifications, but rather on a series of negative attributions, attributions of what one is against, or what one is not. *Not* a foreigner, not a woman, not a person of color—the various positive attributes that were attacked in one way or another during the campaign. Some voters were drawn to this, not just those that came from traditional Republican groups, but independents and Democrats (especially midwestern blue-collar Democrats) who crossed over and voted for Trump. How might we read this development? I believe that we might find one approach to this in the work of Lacan, from 70 years ago, in his paper on *Logical Time and the Assertion of Anticipated Certainty*.[1]

Lacan had something to say about what he termed "collective logic." He stated that individuals situate themselves within groups not on the basis of positive attributions (for example, "I am X because I have some positive attribution of X"). Rather, individuals assimilate into groups on the basis of what he refers to as a negative attribution (for example, "I know what NOT X is"). The example Lacan gives is the following:

> "(1) A man knows what "not a man" is;
> (2) Men recognize themselves among themselves as men;
> (3) I declare myself to be a man for fear of being convinced by men that I am not a man."[2]

Out of anxiety, individuals will rush to declare themselves a member of a group for fear of being left out and rejected by the group. I believe that this logic was in play with many Trump voters. It is a time of anxiety and fear among many in the United States, and people felt that they were being left out and jumped on board with Trump partly out of fear and anxiety to situate themselves under the signifier "American."

The old points of identification based on one's ethnicity, religion, geography or work seem to be weakening somewhat in the United States. Those old points of identification (or, what we might call *semblants* today) were never truly permanent, or as permanent as people believe they are. These points of identification are always changing. But, there had been greater stability in them in past, especially during the great *pax Americana* that reigned from the end of World War 2 through, say, 1980 and the beginning of neo-liberalism. We might think of these identities as like balloons. And if the 1960s to a certain extent cut the moorings holding the balloons down, the winds of global capitalism unleashed over the past few decades are pushing them about here and there. A politics that is based on such points of positive identification may not be as powerful

---

[1] Jacques Lacan, "Logical Time and the Assertion of Anticipated Certainty," *op. cit.* See also Éric Laurent, "Racism 2.0," *op. cit.*

[2] Jacques Lacan, "Logical Time and the Assertion of Anticipated Certainty," *op. cit.*, page 174.

today, especially in a time of great anxiety and social change. And, it may be that in an era of change, the collective logic that Lacan identified in 1946 might better describe collective logic today.[3]

All this said about the logic behind the support for Trump, I would add that the Democratic party was given an opportunity to follow the same collective logic. The campaign of Bernie Sanders was, prior to the general election, perhaps no less a surprise than the Trump primary performance. He was remarkably successful in a way that shocked the Democratic establishment. And he too built his campaign on a negative point of identification. We might say that for Sanders, the Democratic party is a party based on the fact that its members are not the "One Percent." The conflict or antagonism articulated by Sanders was based on a negative assimilation that "what makes America great" are all those who are not in that rarified economic elite, or those advancing the interests of the One Percent. And, it was this negative logic of assimilation that drew some of those most anxious Americans in the same way that Trump did, but with a very different outcome that might have been realized had Sanders faced Trump.

6.2 Bury the Hatchet

Asked about her commitment to running for and again leading the United States House of Representatives as Speaker of the House, Nancy Pelosi replied "It's an urgency I can't resist."[4]

This use of the relatively uncommon (at least, in the United States) word *urgency* of course evokes the upcoming Congress of the New Lacanian School that has that precise title.

This matter of urgency speaks to the increased place of hate and fear in American politics over the past two years, generally ascribed to the politics of Donald Trump (though of course the presence of similar discourse

[3] All this is said quickly, for some identifications, such as race for African Americans, remain strong and very linked to group formation and voting choices, which I suspect is probably a legacy of the greater and continued racism present at various levels of American society.

[4] See https://www.cnn.com/2018/11/08/politics/nancy-pelosi-house-speaker-cnntv/index.html, accessed on December 28, 2022.

in Europe and elsewhere speak to the fact that this is a global phenomenon—we are more globally connected than ever, in the flows of capital and labor and even ideology as well, in spite of efforts to stem that flow). But, of course, that said, the hatred is no less evident on the side of many on the left, who hate Trump and Republicans with no less passion. Those who grieve the loss of civil discourse in American politics—which indeed was somewhat characteristic at times of Washington, DC, during the period of post-War stability through, say, the late 1960's or the 1980's, depending on where one makes the historical break point—are quick to forget the conflict and hatred and fear that characterized part of the 1950's and the activities of Joe McCarthy and which indeed has been an intermittent feature of American politics for a long time, as documented most forcefully by Richard Hofstadter, apropos the Goldwater campaign, in his 1964 essay "The Paranoid Style in American Politics."[5] Indeed, our Congress was quite wild exactly a century before the 1950's in the 1850's with Representatives showing up in chambers armed with guns and knives, all part of the tensions and conflict associated with slavery.[6]

As Claudia Iddan referenced in her very sharp text on the judiciary and Israel,[7] the formation of a group—in her case, talking about a nation, but this could apply as well to a political party—is noted by Jacques Lacan in *Seminar XVII* to be a function of segregation, an act of segregation based upon hatred of the other, those outside of the group (see too here the remarkable conclusion of Lacan's early text on "Logical Time and the Assertion of Anticipated Certainty" for an earlier formulation of this concept, one that I found helpful in an analysis of the 2016 US presidential election[8]).

One conclusion that we might draw from Lacan's work on groups is, of course, that groups are inherently Imaginary constructs and thus, as

---

[5] Published in a book of the same name, but available in the original *Harper's* essay at https://harpers.org/archive/1964/11/the-paranoid-style-in-american-politics/ on December 28, 2022.

[6] See the work of Joanne Freeman, summarized in her *New York Times* opinion piece: "The Violence at the Heart of Our Politics," *New York Times*, September 8, 2018, accessed on December 28, 2022, at https://www.nytimes.com/2018/09/07/opinion/sunday/violence-politics-congress.html.

[7] "Are There Judges?" *Lacanian Review Online*, #103, November 11, 2018, accessed on December 28, 2022, at http://www.thelacanianreviews.com/are-there-judges/.

[8] See the first text in Chap. 6 of this book.

such, are logically based on some form of *meconnaissance*, of misrecognition. I suspect that for some of the left and left political groups, it is a matter of valence: the idealism and hope of various left or progressive agendas hiding some hatred or negative emotion, especially towards the *jouissance* of the Other. We see this most succinctly in a fictional episode of *The West Wing*: the conservative character Ainsley Hayes working in the otherwise progressive White House puts it best, in an exchange with her liberal co-worker Sam Seaborn in a conversation about gun control:

Sam Seaborn: "It's not about personal freedom, and it certainly has nothing to do with public safety. It's just that some people like guns."

Ainsely Hayes: "Yes, they do. But you know what's more insidious than that? Your gun control position doesn't have anything to do with public safety, and it's certainly not about personal freedom. It's about you don't like people who *do* like guns. You don't like the people. Think about that, the next time you make a joke about the South."[9]

Another rather striking example of this position on the left is the response of some progressives to the act taken in 1965 by Bob Dylan. At the time, Dylan was at the top of the progressive, folk music scene in the United States (and, indeed, many folk musicians were quite progressive in their politics and their political advocacy: e.g., Pete Seeger was a member of the Communist Party). As a very young man in the early 1960's, Dylan erupted on the scene and was seen as the one to carry the torch of Woody Guthrie and Pete Seeger to a new generation. Well, Bob Dylan did not want that *semblant*, he wanted to do what he wanted to do musically and was not interested in this identification. So, wanting to move in a different direction, he "went electric" in 1965, adding the blues guitar player Mike Bloomfield and a few others as a backup band. The global reaction on the part of the left folk scene was striking—hatred, vitriol, accusations that Dylan was Judas—and not just in the United States, but also in his English tours of that period (as documented so well in Martin Scorsese's documentary, *No Direction Home*).

So, what then in politics? In her article, Iddan describes one approach that is not founded on hatred, apropos the judiciary, namely that one must protect human rights for everyone, regardless of affiliation or

[9] Quote accessed on December 28, 2022, at https://www.imdb.com/title/tt0745637/quotes.

identification. This universalism is perhaps one path by which one might transcend groups and the imaginary identifications that come with it. (One might even read this universalism in Lacan's work itself, in *Television*, in his musings on the role of the saint, where he states, "The more saints, the more laughter; that's my principle, to wit, the way out of capitalist discourse—which will not constitute progress, if it happens only for some."[10])

I propose that another path would be to subvert the *semblants* of the group, subversion being, according to Jacques-Alain Miller (in his 2005 radio interviews on France Culture, "Histoires de Psychanalyse"[11]), a properly Lacanian approach to politics. I believe one small example of this is Return Day, celebrated in Georgetown, Delaware.[12] For the past two centuries, on this day, a few days after the election, candidates of both parties drive through town in horse-drawn carriages, then the election results are announced, and then they literally "bury the hatchet," an act I see as inherently subversive of the party identifications, without necessarily dissolving them.

---

[10] Jacques Lacan, *Television, op. cit.*, page 16.

[11] Audio links to the radio series "Histoires de . . . psychanalyse" on France Culture were posted on the lacan.com website at https://www.lacan.com/millerlecture.htm, accessed on December 28, 2020. The remarks on politics were made in the session "Anguille en politique" on June 23, 2005.

[12] See Randall Chase, "Delaware politicians bury a hatchet in post-election ritual," *Washington Post*, November 8, 2018. Accessed on December 28, 2022, at https://www.yahoo.com/news/delaware-politicians-gather-ritual-post-election-healing-225815658.html.

7

Immigration

Abstract The United States of America has a long history of claiming to welcome immigrants. In fact, the very term for this—"melting pot"—was derived from a description of European immigrants melting together in taking on the new identification of American as far back as 1782. That said, the story of immigration in the United States has a rather more conflictual dimension to it, as successive waves of immigrants were not always received warmly into the country. A story of Hellenophobia—of hatred to the early twentieth century Greek immigrants—built upon a disgust with the lifestyle of the Greek immigrants and wish on the part of some that Greeks not intermingle with the established Americans was the basis of riots against Greek-Americans in Omaha, in 1909, a series of riots, precipitating events, and background of labor unrest that prefigured race riots during the Red Summer that also affected Omaha in 1919.

Keywords Immigrant experience • Melting pot • Hellenophobia • Red Summer • Race riots

The issue of immigration was on the agenda of a meeting held in 2018 in Italy, organized by the European schools of the World Association of Psychoanalysis. Illegal immigration was a pressing political issue in Europe at

T. Svolos, *Culture and Politics on the Couch*, The Palgrave Lacan Series,
https://doi.org/10.1007/978-3-031-61365-4_7

that moment and our European colleagues wished to address the issue. I was asked to contribute a preparatory text, presumably to address the issue of immigration in the United States. I highlighted the threat of the immigrant in both the libidinal and economic domains as this played out historically in the Greek-American immigrant experience in the United States.

7.1 Stranger in a Melting Pot

I live in the United States, in Omaha, Nebraska.[1] All my grandparents emigrated to the United States, about one hundred years ago, from Greece. While up to that point, the United States was largely settled by Northern Europeans (especially British, Scots, Dutch, Germans and later Scandinavians and Irish), the turn of the century marked the moment of Southern European emigration to the US, from Italy and Greece.

The dominant story of immigration in the United States has always been that of the *melting pot*, in which people from diverse countries assimilate into the society and culture of the United States. This was first articulated by J. Hector St. John de Crevecoeur in his *Letters from an American Farmer*, where he wrote, in 1782, that "What attachment can a poor European emigrant have for a country where he had nothing? The knowledge of the language, the love of a few kindred as poor as himself, were the only cords that tied him; his country is now that which gives him his land, bread, protection, and consequence; *Ubi panis ibi patria* is the motto of all emigrants. What, then, is the American, this new man? He is either an European or the descendant of an European; hence that strange mixture of blood, which you will find in no other country. I could point out to you a family whose grandfather was an Englishman, whose wife was Dutch, whose son married a French woman, and whose present four sons have now four wives of different nations. He is an American, who, leaving behind him all his ancient prejudices and manners, receives new ones from the new mode of life he has embraced, the new

[1] This text was a preparatory text for the February 24, 2018, Forum "Lo Straniero: Inquietudine Soggettiva e Disagio Sociale nel Fenomeno Dell'Immigrazone in Europa" held in Turin, sponsored by la movida Zadig.

government he obeys, and the new rank he holds. He becomes an American by being received in the broad lap of our great Alma Mater. Here individuals of all nations are melted into a new race of men, whose labours and posterity will one day cause great changes in the world."[2]

By all accounts, two generations after my grandparents arrived, in most ways, I was rather fully melted into the United States. And, yet, for me, I have always felt myself, in a subtle way, something of a stranger in the United States. Perhaps that did not have to do with my heritage as a Greek. After all, to be a stranger can manifest itself in many ways, above all the sense in which a speaking being may be a stranger to himself ("Struggling with confusion, disillusionment too; Can turn a man into a shadow, crying out from pain; Through his nightmare vision, he sees nothing, only well; Blind with the beggar's mind, he's but a stranger; But a stranger to himself." *John Barleycorn Must Die*, Traffic, 1970). Indeed, further, I recall well in a course I took in college on T. S. Elliot and the French Symbolist poets encountering this line from Rimbaud's May 13, 1871, letter to Georges Izambard, that resonated with me: "*Je est un autre*," [I is an other], an evocative sentence that pre-figures, in a sense, the Unconscious itself (as Lacan put it in *Seminar II*, regarding Rimbaud's sentence: "poets, as is well known, don't know what they're saying, yet they still manage to say things before anyone else."[3]). I recall especially the shock of the linguistic form that Rimbaud used—the use of the third person conjugation of "to be" instead of the first person form—which now in retrospect for me is an allusion to the great theme of Otherness (e.g., strangeness) that Freud borrowed from Gustav Fechner for his concept of the Unconscious and that Jacques-Alain Miller refined in his elucidation of Lacan's notion of *extimacy*, or, the way in which that which is most intimate for the speaking being is in fact what might be most external, strange, and foreign to him or her.

Yet, that said: there is a way in which this sense of strangeness will get figured for any speaking being, or, the way in which the strangeness will

[2] J. Hector St. John De Crevecoeur, *Letters from an American Farmer and Sketches of Eighteenth-Century America*, Penguin Classics, 1981, pp. 69–70.

[3] Arthur Rimbaud, *Rimbaud: Complete Works, Selected Letters*, Chicago, University of Chicago Press, 1966, page 304. Jacques Lacan, *The Seminar of Jacques Lacan: Book II: The Ego in Freud's Theory and in the Technique of Psychoanalysis*, W. W. Norton, 1988, page 7.

draw upon the history of any speaking being—including that of his or her parents and grandparents. And, indeed, I recall from my youth that while my familial ancestors were able to make it in the US, there were allusions to struggles and difficulties that they faced as a function of being strangers and the way in which they were seen as somehow lesser people due to their Greek heritage. I recall particularly one memorable conversation from many years ago, around the time that I—who grew up on the East Coast—moved to Omaha. I was talking with a family friend who worked as a United States Senate staffer, a Greek-American well connected in the Greek-American diaspora. He made an allusion to the fact that Omaha was a historically dangerous place for Greeks to move to, but did not elaborate further and the conversation quickly moved on.

Having lived in Omaha now for twenty years, I must say that I feel no burden or mistreatment as a Greek-American at all. (Though, interestingly, as someone raised in the more dynamic and intense conversational style of the East Coast, I have had to make some adjustment to the Midwestern discursive style—more polite, less emotional or aggressive, as it were. This speaks to an issue perhaps particular to the United States, namely that "strangeness" may have as much to do with regionality or even individual state identifications as ethnic background.) So, no sense of strangeness for me as a Greek. And yet, researching this many years later, I learned of the very particular position of Omaha as one of the historically important sites of *Hellenophobia* in the United States.[4] The situation in Omaha was as follows: in February 1909, a Greek man was taking English lessons from a woman who was not Greek. The man and the woman were arrested, and, in the course of the arrest, the Greek shot and killed the officer. A series of meetings were organized by local politicians, one politician allegedly stating that "The blood of an American is on the hands of these Greeks and some method should be adopted to avenge his death and rid the city of this class of persons."[5] A mob of several thousand people formed and attacked Greek Town in South Omaha, beating the Greek Americans, burning their homes and businesses, and

[4] See https://en.wikipedia.org/wiki/Anti-Greek_sentiment and also https://en.wikipedia.org/wiki/Greek_Town_riot for specific information on Omaha as references for the account below.

[5] See also "South Omaha Mob Wars on the Greeks," *New York Times*, Feb 22, 1909, page 1.

allegedly killing one Greek American boy. At the time, there were several thousand Greek Americans in Omaha and most all left the city. Some of the language about the Greeks refers to them as living in "unsanitary" conditions and as having "insulted" women. I will come back to this issue of "dirtiness" later. But, another key to the whole incident is the context for the riot. At the time, the railroads and meatpacking were major industries in Omaha, and several thousand Greeks came to Omaha pursuing that work. The packinghouses were largely unionized with workers who were not Greek, and the owners hired Greeks to break some strikes that were ongoing at the time. So, there were two issues at stake here—one relating to the contact between a Greek man and a woman who was not Greek—the stranger threatening to take away the woman—and the second relating to the Greek as stranger taking away the livelihood of the non-Greek.

What is interesting about the Omaha riot against the Greeks is that it prefigures a later riot, in 1919. At the time, with the Greeks largely gone, the meatpacking plants had taken to hiring African-Americans as strikebreakers. There were significant labor actions in many places in the United States in 1919, and Omaha was no exception. In September 1919, an African-American man, Will Brown, was alleged to have raped a white woman.[6] The evidence was apparently weak, but nonetheless, a mob formed and stormed the Courthouse, demanding the release of the Brown to the mob. Unable to get him initially, they set to burning the Courthouse, and they also took custody of and lynched the Omaha Mayor (hung on a lamp post), who was eventually saved. The mob was set on destroying the Courthouse and all the officials and officers within, and the officials eventually turned over Will Brown to the mob, who killed him brutally. The similarities to the Greek riots are striking. In both cases, a group of people (Greek-Americans, African-Americans) are identified as strangers, come to Omaha for work. Ethic and racial tension develop as the strangers walk the line of striking meat packers. An allegation is made of sexual contact between a male stranger and a female non-stranger, leading to mob violence.

[6] See https://en.wikipedia.org/wiki/Omaha_race_riot_of_1919 for this account.

It is in the context of this personal background and this heritage of mine from which I heard the comments alleged to have been made by the current American President about the desirability of certain Northern European immigrants and the undesirability of others, allegedly those from "shithole countries."[7] I immediately recognized that for some in the United States, that is how my ancestors—my grandparents and my other relatives—were seen; that is how the Greek-Americans in Omaha were seen a century ago, as dirty and unsanitary. But, in addition to this signification of the other, the stranger, as unsanitary or shitty, it must be noted as well the sense of fear that underlies the naming—the semblant—assigned to the stranger. It is a fear of loss—loss of the woman to the stranger, as we saw in the Omaha riots against both the Greek and African-Americans, and also loss of livelihood, jobs, access to money. I suppose sometimes the ingredients in the melting pot just don't always mix.

I wonder further how much this might play into the current plight of the Greeks in Europe. Certainly, the characterization of contemporary European Greeks as lazy, corrupt, and willing to live in lesser (unsanitary?) conditions has been a part of the way in which events of the last decade have been constructed in public discourse (always in contrast to the industrious and hard-working Germans). But, as Yannis Varoufakis has argued in his recent memoir of his brief period as the Greek Finance Minister, *Adults in the Room*, the culprit, in a sense, may be less the Greeks than the establishment financial institutions (European Central Bank, International Monetary Fund) who exhibited poor decision-making in their loans to Greece and, at a certain point, very conscious decisions about granting loans which would likely never get repaid, but which, as institutions "too big to fail," as we say of Wall Street, led to the brutal regime of austerity on the Greeks.[8] One of the interesting conclusions of Varoufakis, however, is that the Greeks themselves may have been innocent bystanders, the formal recipients of a message that was really intended for Spain, Portugal and ultimately France.

---

[7] Kimon de Greef and Sewell Chan, "Trump Comments, Infuriating Africans, May Set Back U.S. Interests," *New York Times*, January 15, 2018.

[8] Yannis Varoufakis, *Adults in the Room: My Battle with the European and American Deep Establishment*, Farrar, Straus, and Giroux, 2017.

8

Climate Change

Abstract The phenomenon of climate change and human responses to it are indeed massive and discussion of these subjects might incorporate ecology, energy science, public health, geography, political science, geology, finance, government, medicine, and many fields. The unique contribution of psychoanalytic discourse to these debates is to isolate the subjective factors in the way people frame the subject. The "stance" to climate change or the sense of urgency to issues of the individual or social response to it are all reflective of a particular way in which the person will frame the issue—both the easy to frame aspects and also more importantly those less apparent to the person, those more opaque to human representation. In the first paper in this chapter, a comparison is made between the interpretive process of psychoanalysis—taking something that causes anxiety and putting it into words—and the reading effect of a recent near-future novel of climate change, Kim Stanley Robinson's *Ministry for the Future*. The second paper in the chapter puts attention on a certain idealism that features strongly in how some represent nature.

Keywords Climate change • Climate anxiety • Near-future science fiction • Hyperobjects • Kim Stanley Robinson • *Ministry for the Future* • Human impact on the environment • Great Pacific Garbage Patch • Eco-psychology

T. Svolos, *Culture and Politics on the Couch*, The Palgrave Lacan Series,
https://doi.org/10.1007/978-3-031-61365-4_8

The first text on climate change responds both to the phenomenon of climate change that is receiving increasing attention as well as a 2021 challenge from Spanish colleague Gustavo Dessal for psychoanalysts to step up. Dessal claimed that psychoanalysis was ignoring the phenomenon, and I chose to pick up the gauntlet that he threw down.

The second text was prepared as a preparatory text for the 2023 Congress of the New Lacanian School on "Discontent and Anxiety in the Clinic and in Civilization" on the request of a European colleague for another text on climate change. My intent was to highlight that nature, unlike human institutions, is not ordered, but inherently disordered. It was not published because its length exceeded the parameters of preparatory texts.

8.1 Psychoanalysis, Science Fiction, and Climate Change

In November 2021, Madrid psychoanalyst Gustavo Dessal challenged the psychoanalysts of the Lacanian orientation to take account of climate change, which he referred to as a "blind spot" in the discourse of Lacanian psychoanalysis.[1]

When it comes to the issue of climate change and the possible fate or future for the earth, for our planet, what might a psychoanalyst have to say about this from the perspective of psychoanalysis? What does psychoanalysis have to say about this whole set of issues that cover climate, geology, science, policy, media, international affairs, ecology and all the other discourses that address the topic?

A starting point might be the recognition that, for a psychoanalyst, our focus is not so much on the scientific or political issues as such, but rather on how they are spoken of, to us, as psychoanalysts in our consulting rooms, or, perhaps more broadly, how we hear them or read them discussed and presented in public discourse.

Certainly, some patients talk about climate change and global warming, and my first observation about it is that they are most often spoken of in the register of anxiety. Some analysands of mine speak of

[1] Gustavo Dessal, "Our Blind Spot," *Lacanian Review Online*, #320, November 26, 2001.

anxiety—and, at times, panic and anguish—when they address the issue of climate change and the future of our planet. That, too, is what others who work in psychology and mental health seem to be hearing as well. A recent headline from the front page of the *New York Times* highlighted this: "Anxiety Over Climate Change Lands on the Therapist's Couch."[2]

For the Lacanian psychoanalyst, this anxiety or anguish signals that we have entered the realm of the real. While this is being described, obviously, with words—the affect of anxiety and anguish is a signal of the real, which Lacan described as the only affect that is not deceptive.[3] We are dealing with something here that is exceeding the ability of language and the symbolic order to capture, at least for some subjects, and that affects them differently.

And, we see an interesting resonance of this with at least one of the recent philosophical approaches to the phenomenon of climate change, as articulated by Timothy Morton in his book *Hyperobjects: Philosophy and Ecology after the End of the World.*[4] Morton's hypothesis is that phenomena such as climate change are hyperobjects, in that they transcend our frameworks for understanding what constitutes an object in the world—they are, to use Freud's term, *uncanny* and do not behave like other objects. Or, we might say that they defy the frameworks we use for the depiction of everyday objects. They defy, for example, our usual sense of space and time.

It is interesting to note that one of the production companies for the 2021 movie satire *Don't Look Up*, that was, at least in part, intentionally scripted as an allegorical commentary on the global response to climate change, is named Hyperobject Industries.[5]

So—my first conclusion is that in the consulting room and also in more public philosophical and even popular movie discourses, we are dealing with something of the real, something difficult to get a handle on,

---

[2] Ellen Barry, "Anxiety Over Climate Change Lands on the Therapist's Couch," New *York Times*, Feb. 7, 2022, page A1.

[3] See Jacques Lacan, *The Seminar of Jacques Lacan: Book X: Anxiety, op. cit.*

[4] Timothy Morton, *Hyperobjects: Philosophy and Ecology after the End of the World*, Minneapolis, University of Minnesota Press, 2013.

[5] See https://en.wikipedia.org/wiki/Don%27t_Look_Up. See also https://en.wikipedia.org/wiki/Hyperobject_Industries. Both sites accessed on February 13, 2022.

something that isn't working, something maybe outside of our usual laws or frameworks for objects, something that is impossible to represent—all attributes of the Lacanian real.

So how do we "catch hold" or "get a handle on" this real, to use Lacan's terms on how the psychoanalyst might approach the real?[6]

Well, as psychoanalysts, we have many ways we conceptualize the approach to the real from the clinical perspective of psychoanalysis, a discourse on the subject that may well work for us psychoanalysts deeply steeped in our discourse, in our "parlance," as Jacques-Alain Miller puts it,[7] but a discourse that is, however, hard to describe for those without the experience of psychoanalysis and long study of its works.

Putting aside psychoanalysis, for a minute, I argue that we also have a literary form that does this exceedingly well, namely—science fiction. Take, for example, the work of Kim Stanley Robinson more generally, and, on the subject of climate change, his most recent book, *The Ministry for the Future*, more particularly.[8]

Ministry for the Future is a "near-future" novel, a novel set a decade or two or three in the future, on earth, sometime not far from now. In the story, the earth has warmed up further than where it is now, and the novel is the story of the consequences of this warming (mass death, extinction of some forms of life, and so forth) and the responses across the globe (on a local, national, as well as international scale) to the change, including efforts to confront it and turn the direction of warming around. I would like to highlight several features of the work.

First, it presents something (global warming) that can be described, can be put into words, can be placed in a spatial and temporal frame. Climate change is no longer uncanny, but very much documented. While there is enormous suffering in the story from the effects of climate change as well, I assert that, discursively, we are no longer as much in the realm

[6] "Catch hold": Jacques Lacan, *The Seminar of Jacques Lacan: Book XXIV: L'insu que sait de l'une bévue, s'aile à mourre* (1976–1977), Unpublished translation by Dan Collins from the French as published in *Ornicar?*. Session of March 8, 1977. "Handle": Jacques Lacan, *The Seminar of Jacques Lacan: Book XXIII: The Sinthome* (1975–1976), *op. cit.*, page 101. For development of this, see Chapter 2, "An Easy Handle on the Real," in Thomas Svolos, *The Aims of Analysis: Miami Seminar on the Late Lacan, op. cit.*, 2019.

[7] Jacques-Alain Miller, "The Real Unconscious," *op. cit.*, page 29.

[8] Kim Stanley Robinson, *The Ministry for the Future*, New York, Orbit/Hachette Book Group, 2020.

of the real. Robinson's words make climate change an ordinary object, which can be confronted. As a psychoanalyst, I would say that Robinson found a way to "catch hold" of this real through the very act of putting it into words, of symbolizing it, in this long story.

His approach, however, is not a fairy tale—there is no idealistic "solution" to the problem. Indeed, just to step back a bit from this novel, let me remark that science fiction in general is, in some ways, a challenging literary form for the psychoanalyst. Fredric Jameson has rightly highlighted that one of the key dimensions of science fiction is the way in which so many works in the genre work within the tradition of utopian literature.[9] On first glance, one certainly could construct a psychoanalytic approach to utopian literature or science fiction that would be very skeptical. After all, when it comes to politics (one dimension of utopia), there is a strong anti-idealism in psychoanalysis: according to Jacques-Alain Miller, psychoanalysis is inherently skeptical of both left and right idealisms, and utopian thought certainly can be figured as a form of idealism.[10] That said, I think that there is another way to approach this issue. In a recent profile of Robinson in *The New Yorker*, Robinson describes his work as "anti-anti-utopian."[11] For me, this description by Robinson opens up a very different perspective on this literature. For starters, so much "anti-utopian" discourse itself is a form of conservative idealism (including especially those structured on notions of human nature and so forth). I believe that Robinson's novel is skeptical perhaps of both any idealistic solution to climate change and also the idealistic denial of climate change—to take my initial comment above, the novel works in the register of the symbolic (in the Lacanian discourse), or one might say "materialistic" (in the Marxist discourse), rather than in the register of the imaginary or the realm of the idealistic.

---

[9] Fredric Jameson, *Archaeologies of the Future: The Desire Called Utopia and Other Science Fictions*, London, Verso, 2007.

[10] Jacques-Alain Miller, "L'anguille en politique," Radio broadcast on France Culture, June 22, 2005. See also Thomas Svolos, "The Body Politic," Chapter 8 of *Twenty-first Century Psychoanalysis*, *op. cit.*, pages 93–102.

[11] Joshua Rothman, "Can Science Fiction Wake Us Up to Our Climate Reality? Kim Stanley Robinson's novels envision the dire problems of the future—but also their solutions," *The New Yorker*, January 24, 2022, page 34.

We might approach this from another angle as well: the "real" of climate change is, for some, an old-style real, the real of nature, the real written in the stars, and a real that is, in its way, a necessity. Nature is immutable. It is a catastrophe that is inevitable. It lives, in Aristotelean modal logic, the zone of Necessity. It will happen, and there is nothing that we can do about this. This is a discursive frame of the situation that is very familiar in the realm of clinical practice of psychoanalysis—people often believe in the inevitability of their lives, their situations, and so forth.

Part of the effect of Robinson's work, however, is to move this from the realm of Necessity to the realm of Possibility—the necessity of a catastrophic future (as, for example, in *Don't Look Up*) is transformed into a difficult future, one with conflict and loss, but one that is not catastrophic, or world ending. This discursive effect of his work grants agency to humans, opens a place for subjectivity (which is, of course, linked to the symbolic), for choice. Some humans might choose to act. And, interestingly, this is indeed one of the ways we might figure psychoanalysis itself—the necessity of a certain imperative, master signifiers, a fundamental fantasy, or possibly even a certain mode of *jouissance* gets transformed into a possibility of something different, in the opening of a subjective space for desire.

8.2 A Filthy and Disordered World

Ten years ago, Jacques-Alain Miller addressed the theme of nature, not today's nature, but nature in antiquity and in the Christian era, in the context of a talk on the real. Miller noted that "Nature was the name of the real when there was no disorder in the real. When nature was the name of the real you could say, as Lacan did, that the real always returns to the same place. Only in this epoch, in this epoch in which the real disguised itself as nature, the real appeared as the most evident, the most elevated, manifestation of the very concept of order."[12] Nature, for the

[12] Jacques-Alain Miller. "The Real for the 21st Century." In World Association of Psychoanalysis (Eds.). *Scilicet: A Real for the 21st Century*, Paris, NLS Publication., 2014, pages 25–36.

ancients in the West, was ordered, it returned to the same place because the ancient human perception of nature was that it was ordered, everything was assigned a place and there was a logic of how it was structured. In this text, Miller goes on to note that even in the Christian era in the West, this was preserved, in that it was God who provided that very order, who assigned places and so forth.

Miller approaches this topic from the perspective of the real. My sense of this lecture is that Miller brings this point about the perspective of nature to demonstrate something not about nature, but about the real, most notably how we have entered now into a new moment of the real, where the real is no longer ordered, as it was, but disordered or, to use a phrase we hear often, lawless, this property linked to the thesis of generalized madness. And, for Miller, it is a change in our human world—which he briefly surveys, highlighting the rise of the discourse of science and the discourse of capitalism—that brings this about.

With great sympathy for Miller's argument, I wonder if we might not turn the focus of this not to the real, but rather to nature itself. And, furthermore, I would suggest that what might be of interest here is not nature as such, not nature itself, or, nature as an object of scientific study (but, of course, science can only take up pieces of nature and, in doing so, nature as a whole is lost). What I am interested here is more the human concept of nature, the fantasy of nature, the ideology of nature even, how nature is spoken of in the most general sense.

The human idea of nature in the ancient world and during the height of the Christian era is that nature was ordered. The semblant of the Name-of-the-Father was very strong, in various forms, and we perceived nature as ordered because of our fantasy. Our knowledge of nature, in the pre-scientific era, was always organized by a fantasy of *rapport*, as Lacan argued at various points in *Seminar XX*.[13] Nature was not only ordered, but was a place of ideals, of beauty. With the disenchantment of the world and, as Miller identifies it, the rise of capitalism and science, we are left with a different world, described in other discourses these days as the Anthropocene, the world as affected by and altered by humans, with human-caused climate change one, but only one, of the effects of humans

[13] Jacques Lacan. *The Seminar of Jacques Lacan: Book XX, Encore 1972–1973, op. cit.*

on this world. While denied by some on the right side of the political spectrum (at least in the United States), many people today speak of a disordered and damaged nature, one whose weather is remarkably unstable (severe droughts followed by record shattering precipitation on the West Coast; generalized warming, but also remarkable periods of colder than average weather; increased number of tornadoes and hurricanes and novel extreme weather events such as derechos; and so forth). In the popular media in the United States, we can also find representations of filthy and unclean nature—visual depictions of the results of practices like strip mining for coal; or, landscapes of burnt vegetation and buildings immediately after a large fire; or, pictures of trash and refuse in even the most remote places; or, reports of microplastics even now in rainwater; or, stories on how the overwhelming majority of even properly recycled plastics ends up in landfills—a discouraging fact to even the most ecologically dedicated citizen.

This is the use I make of what Jacques Lacan states in this passage in "The Third," when he says that "we are not lacking in proofs that this *monde* . . . is clearly not *monde*, but *immonde*, filthy."[14] Nature, the world, is no longer constructed or seen or represented as the beautiful and ordered world of the ancient world or the Christian world, but rather a disordered, filthy world. And, this is our doing, the impact of human action on the world. This view, while a dominant one today in American discourse, has its own history. Even Thomas Jefferson, in his diary, noted concerns that "'A change in our climate . . . is taking place very sensibly. Both heats and colds are becoming much more moderate within the memory even of the middle-aged. Snows are less frequent and deep' and 'The elderly inform me that the earth used to [but no longer] be covered by snow for about three months in every year.'"[15]

This social discourse of discontent with nature, with disorder and filthiness of the world, is also interesting for what it doesn't take into account. There can be striking paradoxes in how people view nature today. For example, many in the United States will look upon strip mining (for coal)

[14] Jacques Lacan. "The Third." *The Lacanian Review*, Issue 7, Spring 2019, Page 104.

[15] Thomas Jefferson, quoted in Peter Frankopan. *The Earth Transformed: An Untold History*. New York. Alfred A. Knopf. 2023. Frankopan's work is a valuable global, historical survey of human action on and perception of nature.

as a horrible practice, one which deforests the environment, pollutes streams, leads to loss of animal life, and results in an aesthetically unappealing, "filthy" environment. Indeed, photos of the results of strip mining are vital in building the political pressure to end the practice through governmental action. To me, there is a certain irony here, in that the same person might look at a photo of a Greek island and declare it among the most beautiful natural places. Yet, that topography and landscape that is admired so much today was a result of a major program of deforestation in the ancient world, which led to the erosion of topsoil across large parts of Greece and a radical change in the ability of the land to support vegetation and animal (and human) life.[16] Nature adopted to the deforestation and erosion, and new forms of plants and animal life came to occupy this topography and terrain so altered by deforestation. I do not find or hear discontent, disgust and anxiety linked to the perception of the hills of Greece like the hills of West Virginia, a center of strip mining in the United States. I will want to come back to the question of the impact of this on perceived anxiety.

First, I want to discuss another example. Garbage is, in a way, the very definition of filth, and many find the presence of garbage in nature a source of great concern. One of the greatest examples (literally) of this is what is known as the Great Pacific Garbage Patch, which is a massive flotsam of floating plastic waste collected by ocean currents in the Pacific Ocean into an 80,000 ton mass (they are present in other oceans as well—the Pacific's is the largest). A recent study reported that this Garbage Patch is, apparently, teaming with life—invertebrates of 46 species growing and reproducing on this man-made plastic garbage dump, including coastal organisms that were hypothesized to have been introduced into it from the 2011 Japanese tsunami that otherwise do not survive in salt water.[17] A study author, apparently, noted that "they're having a blast."[18] I do not mean to suggest that human pollution is not a

[16] See, for example, J. Donald Hughes and J. V. Thirgood. "Deforestation, Erosion, and Forest Management in Ancient Greece and Rome." *Journal of Forest History*. Vol. 26, No. 2. April 1982, pages. 60–75.

[17] Nidhi Subbaraman. "Pacific Ocean Garbage Patch Is Bursting With Life." *Wall Street Journal*, April 17, 2023.

[18] *Ibid.*

problem causing direct damage to marine vegetation and animal life that we should mitigate, but merely to highlight how we often place our attention on what is disturbing to us, what is disgusting to us, as a result of human action. We often place less attention on how nature adopts to these changes, in ways that can be surprising or even beautiful (such as the deforested Greek islands).

And, to me, this gets to the issue in "The Third" of the link that Jacques Lacan makes between the filthy universe and our anxiety. Lacan links anxiety to "the presentiment that comes to reduce us to our bodies. It is the feeling that arises from the presentiment that we are being reduced to our body."[19] I assert that when viewing the natural world of Greece, humans delight in the semblants that they make of that natural world, that landscape, the bushes, the shapes of the hills, and so forth. But, encountering the landscape of countless acres recently strip-mined, something of the filthiness that is felt is linked to an awareness of the body that is, I believed, caused by a perceived threat on the body by the environment itself. I do not fear for my body walking the hillsides of Greece as I do in strip-mined West Virginia. I would hazard a guess that that too might be the reaction to the story of marine life thriving in the Great Pacific Garbage Patch. The study author described that "Anemones like to protect themselves with grains of sand, Dr. Egger said, but out in the garbage patch they are covered in seed-like microplastics. Squeeze an anemone and the shards spew out, he said: 'They're all fully loaded with plastic on the outside and inside.'"[20] My sense is that some of the disturbance felt in reading that is linked to the awareness of possibility that the reader's own body could be loaded with microplastics, the "presentiment" as Lacan put it. The title of the article featured on the front page of the "Sunday Opinion" section of the *New York Times* spelled this out: "To Be Human Is to Contain Plastic: maybe this has been our fate all along: to achieve final communion with our own garbage."[21]

But, I don't think that this notion of the world as filthy or disturbing, while certainly more common now and most often linked to the effects

---

[19] Jacques Lacan, "The Third," *op. cit.*, page 104.

[20] Nidhi Subbaraman. "Pacific Ocean Garbage Patch Is Bursting With Life." *Op. cit.*

[21] Mark O'Connell. "What Are the Plastic Particles in Our Bodies Doing to Us." *The New York Times*. April 23, 2023. Page SR6.

of human action in the world, is necessarily linked only to the Anthropocene world of today. Think, for example, of the fear of a meteor hitting the earth. Or, for a different example: I can recall the first time I experienced the desert in the American West. I had flown into Phoenix, Arizona, and was driving on a highway to Sedona. I have done that drive since and found the landscape interesting and enjoyable to watch. But, I recall my sense on that first trip—a mild anxiety surveying the sand and cactuses and spare vegetation on the side of the highway. This anxiety was linked to that very sentiment, to take up Lacan's word, of being reduced to my body—I recall thinking what it would be like to be out there, in the heat, with no water. I remember thinking that it was no surprise that the non-natives (obviously, this was and is a different matter for the Native Americans who knew how to live there) did not want to live in the desert in great numbers. We brought water and electricity to the desert in the West, and the city of Phoenix is now the fifth largest metropolitan area in the United States. But, that anxiety has returned now on a social level, as an imminent crisis of water shortage in the American West is now upon us.

9

Race

Abstract After George Floyd was murdered in the United States in 2020, some Americans embraced the decentralized social movement, Black Lives Matter, that was established first in 2013 to address racism in the United States. At a moment when some in the United States have emphasized a disengagement of young people in social and political matters, the protests and other activities in the name of Black Lives Matter demonstrate a high level of engagement of a diverse group of citizens in social matters. Furthermore, at a moment of general acceptance of a decline of importance in what Lacan called the symbolic order—in a sense of named law or principle, one might say—Black Lives Matter protests highlighted a commitment to a set of words, a set of principles, that formed a mandate for those involved.

Keywords Black Lives Matter • George Floyd • Racism • Antiracism • Ibram X. Kendi • Social movement

The following text was written as a response to the killing of George Floyd and the public reaction to that in the United States. The national response to the killing highlighted the fact that we are now in a very different moment of political action than the countercultural movements of the 1960s that Lacan addressed in some texts.

T. Svolos, *Culture and Politics on the Couch*, The Palgrave Lacan Series,
https://doi.org/10.1007/978-3-031-61365-4_9

9.1 Signifiers of Race Matter

In our world, the world of Lacanian psychoanalysis, we sometimes talk about the decline in the power or the impact of the symbolic order as a defining characteristic of our time, and the corollary rise of the importance of the imaginary and the real. This notion echoes others—Lyotard's observations of the decline of the grand narratives; or, the decline of universality (in the name of particularity or even singularity, in Jameson's description of postmodernity, for example); or, the general idea of a decline in the power of ideals in the political or social realm (replaced by a society of "decadence," according to Ross Douthat's analysis, from the a different end of the ideological spectrum).[1]

This decline of ideals or attachment to master signifiers was a feature of Lacan's own approach to looking at the social phenomena of the 1960's, most notably towards the student protests of that era, which he articulated in his seminar published as *The Other Side of Psychoanalysis*. In that seminar, and in particular the appendix of the seminar—a transcript of an encounter that Lacan had with students in 1969—Lacan notes a decline in the protesting youths' sense of ideals into a certain type of mode of enjoyment.[2] For further elaboration on this and what was happening at the time in France, see also the chapters by Éric Laurent and Jacques-Alain Miller in *Jacques Lacan and the Other Side of Psychoanalysis: Reflections on Seminar XVII*.[3]

Now, Lacan, while clearly a product of the Old World, was able to see what was going to develop in the future in what was happening in his present, at this key transitional moment in global history. Some of his observations of that moment—in 1969–1970—were remarkably prescient: the rise of the hold of enjoyment (what we would commonly

[1] Fredric Jameson, "Postmodernism; or, the Cultural Logic of Late Capitalism," *Op. cit.*, pages 53–92. Russ Douthat, *The Decadent Society: How We Became the Victims of Our Own Success*, New York, Simon & Schuster, 2020.

[2] Jacques Lacan, *The Seminar of Jacques Lacan: Book XVII: The Other Side of Psychoanalysis (1969–1970)*, *Op. cit.*, page 197–208.

[3] Jacques-Alain Miller, "On Shame," in *Jacques Lacan and the Other Side of Psychoanalysis: Reflections on Seminar XVII*, *Op. cit.*, pages 11–28; and, Éric Laurent, "Symptom and Discourse," *Op. cit.*, pages 229–253.

speak of as contemporary consumerism); the rise of enjoyment as a spectacle (e.g., reality shows, celebrity culture, even presidential politics in the United States); the power of technology to libidinally connect with people as articulated in his theory of the *lathouses* in *Seminar XVII* (a theory of smartphones before they were even invented); and, a decline in the role of the affect of shame (evident personally and socially and even politically).

But, what about today? In the United States, and now even globally, we are in the midst of a new series of protests that have developed most immediately in response to the killing of George Floyd. While the killing of George Floyd was not an isolated event, but one in a long series of acts of violence and killing of black men by the police in the United States, this one ignited a protest response of a scope that the United States has not seen in fifty years.

Now, while a large social movement like this is diverse and complex (and included some small elements of anarchist actions and looting—understandable in the face of the high unemployment and poverty levels in the country), the most remarkable thing about them is the three signifiers at the focal point of the protests—Black Lives Matter. These are relatively new signifiers, crafted as a hashtag on social media, #BlackLivesMatter, in 2013 as part of a social media response to the acquittal of the man who shot the African-American teen Trayvon Martin in Florida in 2012.[4] These signifiers serve as the point of unification for the very diverse group of Americans—many young people, people of all races—who have come together in a social movement identified with these signifiers, which we also find all over the internet and on posters placed in the windows of homes and businesses across the United States.

What is interesting is that this is not a symbolic identification in the name of some historical ideal, such as a notion of civil rights, which defined the civil rights protests of the 1960s. This is a novel signifier and a new creation—the invention of a signifier that has immense effects (or, to translate this into later Lacanian terminology—this is the creation of a new semblant, which has had effects in the real itself).

And, furthermore, we see a very interesting return of the affect of shame today, which Lacan identified in the 1960s as on the wane. For

[4] See https://en.wikipedia.org/wiki/Black_Lives_Matter, accessed on July 7, 2020.

one of the strengths of the Black Lives Matter protest movement is the way in which the protestors have the function of incarnating the Other itself, as it were, and shaming the country, especially white America, into confronting its implication in the continued racism present today, long after the end of slavery and the end of Jim Crow laws. Indeed, Ibram X. Kendi's *How To Be an Antiracist* is now a bestselling book in the United States, and Kendi's core hypothesis—an assertion we might even format in Greimassian terms, that the 'contradictory' point to racism (non-racism) is closed, not available; one can either adopt positions or ideas that are racist or the 'contrary' position, anti-racism—is a remarkable one that forces the reader to confront their position regarding racism, something happening in social movements like the protests, in conversations across the country, and in organized institutional activities on university campuses and businesses.[5]

So, in contrast to frequent observations that youth, a driving force in the protests in the United States, are disengaged from society and politics, we see just the opposite. Youth are in fact very engaged, in a movement that has already started to have some real impact in the political and social and economic realms. And, furthermore, these protests, in distinction to what Lacan observed of the French protests of the late 1960s, are protests not organized around enjoyment, but rather signifiers, new signifiers and not old ones, that speak to a symbolic ideal that has allowed people to come together and transcend their identities in the name of this cause.

[5] Ibram X. Kendi, *How to Be an Antiracist,* New York, One World, 2019.

10

Psychoanalysis in Culture

Abstract In his autobiography *Born to Run*, Bruce Springsteen writes with a notable sensitivity and awareness of his internal state of mind, his family of origin, and those that he works with or dealt with as he entered into the music business. He is able to interpret his own interests in music and the impact of his family on the ambition that he had for success as a musician and a human being. The acuity of his interpretations may well be linked to the twenty-five years that the musician spent speaking with his psychoanalyst, who he credits as essential in his autobiography.

Keywords Bruce Springsteen • *Born to Run* • Autobiography • Testimony of psychoanalysis

Compared with some of the issues and events addressed in the other chapters, the following chapter is on a lighter note and is intended to draw attention to an unexpected connection of contemporary mass culture with psychoanalysis in the context of a libidinal crisis of a popular American musician. Springsteen's suffering and his account of it are worthy of interpretation and a kind of testimony of an encounter of the musician with psychoanalysis.

T. Svolos, *Culture and Politics on the Couch*, The Palgrave Lacan Series,
https://doi.org/10.1007/978-3-031-61365-4_10

10.1 "The Boss" and Psychoanalysis

In the United States, many Americans within a generation or two of my age—meaning, many Americans—recognize the musician Bruce Springsteen as "The Boss." Springsteen's songwriting, his lyrics, and his marathon, high energy concert performances have, for decades, attracted fans across the country, critical and popular acclaim, and enormous success. He has been at the very top of the pop/rock music industry.

Springsteen recently published an autobiography, titled *Born to Run*, named after his 1975 breakout album.[1] I recently read this book and was immediately struck by the high level of awareness in his writing. To me, his songs have always been straight up with a lyrical quality to them that, however, could have fallen flat, but—coming through in the songs and in his performances—Springsteen's internal sensitivities and external perceptiveness elevate them to something very special in the music world. This same quality of awareness comes through in the book as well, especially the first half or so up to his achievement of fame and major recognition. Indeed, he spends a lot of time very carefully describing his background growing up in a tough, blue-collar part of New Jersey with a stern and difficult father and the way in which he struggled to find both personal and professional identity (a word he uses often) and in which he developed his passion for the guitar, for playing music, and eventually for singing and writing. He writes with this great awareness for what he is experiencing internally, as it were, and also the ways in which his relationships and the world he grew up in impacts his playing, the ways in which he works with his various groups, and the very themes of his songs and albums. One thing he emphasizes is the very determined desire he had—his ambition for himself and for his music.

At one point, he has made it, achieved some serious recognition, and decides that he will travel across the United States—take a road trip—with a close friend. Driving across Texas, he stops in a small town, watches a small-town dance and celebrate one evening, and this, he writes, brings on a deep sense of dread and anguish—"a deeper anxiety than I've ever

[1] Bruce Springsteen, *Born to Run*, New York, Simon & Schuster, 2016.

known."[2] Springsteen is paralyzed. He talks about being, at that point in his life, forced finally to confront something that he had been defending against all his life ("the defenses I built to withstand the stress of my childhood, to save what I had of myself, outlived their usefulness"),[3] something that his passion, his ambition, and his desire was shielding himself from—something he allusively describes through the book as darkness, depression—what strikes me as some piece of the Real. And, at that point in the book, some 300 pages in, he writes that he sought out counsel from his manager, a friend, who finds a professional for him to see in California, and that he is eventually referred to Wayne Myers, a New York psychoanalyst. He writes that he saw his psychoanalyst for twenty-five years: "The results of my work with Dr. Myers and my debt to him are at the heart of this book."[4]

At this point, for me, as a reader, this awareness that I have sensed in the book becomes retroactively much clearer—this is a book written from the vantage point of someone who has gone through a long psychoanalytic experience, and Springsteen's cognizance of his inner world and the world around him (which he writes about with an unarticulated topological frame not unlike the Moebius strip) gives Springsteen the writer, writing about himself, something like that "extra needle on the dial" that Lacan wrote about in *Seminar I* regarding those who go through the psychoanalytic experience and how it affects them—the experience does not remove one's emotions, opinions, musings, biases and so forth, but enhances the person's awareness of all that so he or she don't act out on them.[5] With analysis, one can use one's emotions, opinions, biases and so on as an "extra needle on the dial" to calibrate one's acts and speech, one's engagement with the world. Well, Springsteen writes here with that very extra needle on the very dial of his own life.

Between the Pope and the Boss, it is interesting to read now of the testimonies of global leaders in very different social domains about what they got from talking with a psychoanalyst.

---

[2] *Ibid.*, page 306.

[3] *Ibid.*

[4] *Ibid.*, page 312.

[5] Jacques Lacan, *The Seminar of Jacques Lacan: Book I, Freud's Papers on Technique (1953–1954)*, New York, Norton, 1988, page 32.

Part V

Concluding Theoretical Remarks on Psychoanalysis and Society

I have chosen to close the book with some theoretical remarks on the relationship of the personal with the social and political. As with the first chapter, these remarks are intended to set a framework or logic for how to articulate the connection between the psyche and the outer world and do presuppose some familiarity with Lacanian concepts.

11

The Personal and the Political

Abstract The usual perspective on the relationship of the individual with society or on the relationship of the personal the political fails to take into account the existence of the unconscious. The unconscious—which is both something "within" the individual, but also something "rejected" by the individual and thus not part of conscious thought—has a curious property of at once being internal and external. This topology is enhanced by the additional fact that the substance of the unconscious is also, in fact, taken in from the outside world. In learning a language, one thus takes in not only the vocabulary and the various rules of grammar and syntax, however, but also some unwritten rules of language that have social and political dimensions to them that get woven into the unconscious.

Keywords The personal and the political • Relationship of individual and society • Topology • Unwritten rules of language • The unconscious • Freud's Rat Man case

T. Svolos, *Culture and Politics on the Couch*, The Palgrave Lacan Series,
https://doi.org/10.1007/978-3-031-61365-4_11

I would like to close this book with just a few theoretical comments on the relationship of the personal and the political.[1]

My remarks here will be based on a couple of theoretical points in Lacan's work that highlight issues of the relationship between the individual and society, or the personal and the political. Let's start with Lacan's notion of the Other. Lacan described the Other as that which is faced by the Subject. This language, this terminology has many roots. Certainly, Subject and Other have philosophical roots, but I think as well that an inspiration here for Lacan was drawn from Freud's original description of the unconscious as the "other scene," a phrase he adopted from Fechner.[2] For Lacan, in this phase of his work, in the 1950s and the early 1960s, the Other was the "treasure trove of signifiers" that are determinant for the Subject.[3] The essence of the psychoanalytic experience was cutting through the Imaginary to find the truth at the level of the Symbolic, in this treasure trove of signifiers. This is aligned with Lacan's interest in the work of Levi-Strauss and structuralism and can be understood as this moment where Lacan adopted both Saussurian linguistics and Levi-Straussian structuralism as a way to rewrite Freud, the Freudian unconscious.

The importance of this for the question of the individual and society or the personal and the political has to do with the fact that the Other is filled up with signifiers from the outside world. The most well described example of this can be found in Lacan's reading of the Rat Man case.[4] Lacan gave a seminar on the Rat Man case a couple years before his seminars were transcribed. We do not have a full transcription of his reading

[1] The text in this chapter is based in part on my responses to questions in an interview with Duane Rousselle, published as "Psychoanalysis and Politics: Duane Rousselle Interviews Thomas Svolos," in the Salon section of the e-journal European Journal of Psychoanalysis] on Nov 3, 2022. Accessed at https://www.journal-psychoanalysis.eu/articles/psychoanalysis-and-politics-duane-rouselle--interviews-thomas-svolos/ on December 27, 2023.

[2] Sigmund Freud, "The Interpretation of Dreams," *The Standard Edition of the Complete Psychological Works of Sigmund Freud*, Vol. 5, London, Hogarth, 1953, pages 535–536.

[3] Jacques Lacan, "The Subversion of the Subject and the Dialectic of Desire in the Freudian Unconscious," *Écrits: The First Complete Edition in English*, *op. cit.*, page 692.

[4] For Lacan's reading of the Rat Man, see Jacques Lacan, "The Neurotic's Individual Myth," *Psychoanalytical Quarterly*, *op. cit.* For a reading of the Rat Man case that develops this in more detail, see Thomas Svolos, Chapter 3, *The Aims of Analysis: Miami Seminar on the Late Lacan*, *op. cit.*

of the Rat Man case in his seminar, but we do have a paper Lacan drafted about the case contemporary with his seminar. The paper details how the Rat Man's suffering, his symptom (about the payment for his glasses), and other aspects of his life were all determined, as it were, by the life of his parents, their courtship, and decisions made by his father, especially regarding his choice of a woman and the way in which the father handled responsibilities. All these factors relating to the parental history are outside of the Rat Man in both time and space, but nonetheless inscribed in signifiers that make up the Rat Man's unconscious and are determinant for him. They are the "treasure trove of signifiers" that permit Freud to interpret the symptom and suffering of the Rat Man. Thus, we see here a key aspect of what the Other is in the psychoanalytic sense. It is something that is both outside of the subject, in this case, literally events outside of the Rat Man in terms of space and time, but also something interior to the subject, in the unconscious of the Rat Man. Jacques-Alain Miller adopted a neologism, extimacy, a combination of exterior and intimacy, to describe this aspect of the Other.[5]

I think that the conclusion we can draw from this is that the existence of the unconscious leads to a necessary recognition of some continuity between what we consider our personal experience, our personal space, and the social and political environment around us. This connection or continuity transgresses the usual distinction or boundary that people like to draw between what is personal and what is political or social. Lacan did not believe in this and famously stated in *Seminar XIV* that "the unconscious is politics."[6]

This is not a formulation, such as that of Carl Jung, that recognizes a collective unconscious. The politics in any individual's unconscious are singular for that individual, such as the case with the Rat Man. No one else shares the Rat Man's particular unconscious. In psychoanalysis, the unconscious is always counted and approached one by one.

---

[5] Jacques-Alain Miller, "Extimité" in *Lacanian Theory of Discourse: Subject, Structure and Society*, New York, New York University Press, 1988, pages 74–87.

[6] Jacques Lacan, *The Seminar of Jacques Lacan: Book XIV: The Logic of Fantasy* (1966–1967). Unpublished translation by Cormac Gallagher. Session of May 10, 1967. Accessed on October 24, 2022, at http://www.lacaninireland.com/web/wp-content/uploads/2010/06/14-Logic-of-Phantasy-Complete.pdf. Translation modified by author.

The social and political dimensions of a singular unconscious are a function of the apprenticeship, as Jacques-Alain Miller emphasizes, of the speaking being in taking on language.[7] A speaking being doesn't just learn the rules of languages. In learning language, something beyond the lexicon and the rules of syntax and grammar, gets woven into the unconscious. This is where we find the social and political phenomena incorporated into the unconscious, those things associated with the world of words surrounding the subject as they acquire language. And, indeed, furthermore—in the twenty-first century, it is not now just the cooing of the mother or nursery rhymes or parental commands or parental banter that surround the speaking being, but all the words coming from screens through which many children today learn language. Fred Jameson famously said in our moment of postmodernism, "multinational capital ends up penetrating and colonizing those very precapitalist enclaves (Nature and the Unconscious) which offered extraterritorial and Archimedean footholds for critical effectivity."[8] I believe that this change in the very nature of the Other for subjects today is one of the ways in which we can theorize the way in which subjects are connected with a world constructed through various forms of media. And, further, note that in *Seminar XVII*, Lacan himself had a theory aligned with this: his notion of the produced object, the *lathouse*, replacing the natural traditional part object linked to the body.[9] The unconscious is more connected with society and culture than ever, not just a residue of familial history. (And, indeed, referencing the comment on the penetration of Nature, is not the presence of microplastics in the very air we breathe some sign as well of the process Jameson alludes to?[10])

---

[7] Jacques-Alain Miller, "Les Trumains," accessed online October 13, 2022, at https://congresoamp2020.com/en/articulos.php?sec=el-tema&sub=textos-de-orientacion&file=el-tema/textos-de-orientacion/20-03-02_los-trumanos.html&utm_source=Campa. This is an English translation by Samya Seth of the May 2, 2007, session of Miller's seminar, *The Very Last Lacan*.

[8] Fredric Jameson, *Postmodernism, or, the Cultural Logic of Late Capitalism*, Durham, Duke University Press, 1991, page 49.

[9] See Jacques Lacan, *The Seminar of Jacques Lacan: Book XVII: The Other Side of Psychoanalysis (1969–1970)*, *Op. cit.*, page 162.

[10] John Schwartz, "Where's Airborne Plastic? Everywhere, Scientists Find: There's "no nook or cranny" on the planet where it doesn't end up, the lead researcher on a new study said." *The New York Times*, June 11, 2020, accessed at https://www.nytimes.com/2020/06/11/climate/airborne-plastic-pollution.html?searchResultPosition=8 on December 27, 2023.

I suggest we can also recall Lacan's fascination with topology, in particular, the topological figures of the Mobius strip and the Klein bottle. These topological forms call into question the very notion of inside and outside. The human subject is not a bag with the psyche inside and things outside, as Freud hypothesized at one point.[11] Rather, topologically, we exist with a continuity between the social world, outside, and a subject's inner thoughts and emotions.

This leads me to believe that what people encounter in the analytic experience, both analysand and psychoanalysts, in the unconscious today are at the same time a possible index of what is happening in social experience. I am no sociologist or political scientist, but my observation is that it would be fair to say, as I argued in Chap. 2, we've moved away from universalism and a domination of the Name-of-the-Father, in social and political formation. The symbolic is no longer as strong and dominant as it was, and the imaginary has developed greater autonomy. I think this feature of the psychic life can be found also in the rise of importance of identity in the social and political world. This is just one example of the interesting connections that we might find between the psychic and the social.

Miller explicitly comments on this in his session of his seminar on *The Very Last Lacan*. This is in the session with his discussion of T.S. Eliot's "The Hollow Men" and a reference Miller makes to Lacan's sociology. Miller comments there "what emerges for me from the reading and editing is that Lacan emphasizes the fact that the human being is essentially social. The topology, so apparent in its Borromean and toric splendor, is incessantly lined by a sociology."[12]

It is up to us to find, in any given case, one by one, what that connection might be between the subject and the social or political space around them. The way in which we do this might vary and certainly will depend on the political and social and cultural world surrounding the subject. Part of our work as psychoanalysts is how to decode this on a subjective level, one by one, so that we might mark the political and social at play in the logic of the symptom, the suffering of the subject.

---

[11] Sigmund Freud, "The Ego and the Id," *The Standard Edition of the Complete Psychological Works of Sigmund Freud*, Vol. 19, London, Hogarth, 1962, page 24.

[12] Jacques-Alain Miller, "Les Trumains," *ibid.*

Works Cited

R. W. Apple Jr., "Edmund S. Muskie, 81, Dies; Maine Senator and a Power on the National Scene," *New York Times*, March 27, 1996, accessed at https://www.nytimes.com/1996/03/27/us/edmund-s-muskie-81-dies-maine-senator-and-a-power-on-the-national-scene.html?searchResultPosition=1, on August 24, 2022.

Erich Auerbach, *Mimesis: The Representation of Reality in Western Literature*, Princeton, Princeton University Press, 1953.

Ellen Barry, "Anxiety Over Climate Change Lands on the Therapist's Couch," *New York Times*, Feb. 7, 2022, page A1.

Bible

Marie-Hélène Brousse, "Choix forcé?" *Lacan Quotidien*, #890, May 22, 2020, accessed December 28, 2022, at https://lacanquotidien.fr/blog/wp-content/uploads/2020/05/LQ-890.pdf.

Marie-Hélène Brousse, *The Feminine: A Mode of Jouissance*, New York, Lacanian Press, 2022.

Randall Chase, "Delaware politicians bury a hatchet in post-election ritual," *Washington Post*, November 8, 2018. Accessed on December 28, 2022, at https://www.yahoo.com/news/delaware-politicians-gather-ritual-post-election-healing-225815658.html

T. Svolos, *Culture and Politics on the Couch*, The Palgrave Lacan Series,
https://doi.org/10.1007/978-3-031-61365-4

CNN. https://www.cnn.com/2018/11/08/politics/nancy-pelosi-house-speaker-cnntv/index.html, accessed on December 28, 2022.
Coronavirus Horse Race, accessed at https://www.youtube.com/watch?v=Fn8MxJx_erk on December 26, 2022.
J. Hector St. John De Crevecoeur, *Letters from an American Farmer and Sketches of Eighteenth-Century America*, Penguin Classics, 1981.
Guy Debord, *The Society of the Spectacle*, New York, Zone Books, 1994.
Gustavo Dessal, "Los delincuentes por sentimiento de soledad" published on the Zadig Espana site on May 9, 2020, accessed at https://zadigespana.com/2020/05/09/coronavirus-los-delincuentes-por-sentimiento-de-soledad/ on December 26, 2020.
———, "Our Blind Spot," *Lacanian Review Online*, #320, November 26, 2001.
———, "Reclusions" in *Lacanian Review Online*, issue "COVID series" #87 on May 8, 2020. Accessed at https://www.thelacanianreviews.com/reclusions/ on December 26, 2022.
Russ Douthat, *The Decadent Society: How We Became the Victims of Our Own Success*, New York, Simon & Schuster, 2020.
Michel Foucault, *The Care of the Self: Volume 3 of the History of Sexuality*, New York, Vintage Books, 1988.
———, *The Use of Pleasure: Volume 2 of the History of Sexuality*, New York, Vintage Books, 1990.
Peter Frankopan. *The Earth Transformed: An Untold History*. New York. Alfred A. Knopf. 2023.
Joanne Freeman, "The Violence at the Heart of Our Politics," *New York Times*, September 8, 2018, accessed on December 28, 2022, at https://www.nytimes.com/2018/09/07/opinion/sunday/violence-politics-congress.html
Sigmund Freud, "Beyond the Pleasure Principle," *The Standard Edition of the Complete Psychological Works of Sigmund Freud*, Vol. 18, London, Hogarth, 1955a, pages 7–64.
———, "Civilization and Its Discontents," *The Standard Edition of the Complete Psychological Works of Sigmund Freud*, Vol. 21, London, Hogarth, 1964a, pages 59–148.
———, *Civilization and Its Discontents*, New York, Penguin Classics, 2002.
———, "The Ego and the Id," *The Standard Edition of the Complete Psychological Works of Sigmund Freud*, Vol. 19, London, Hogarth, 1962, page 24.
———, "The Interpretation of Dreams," *The Standard Edition of the Complete Psychological Works of Sigmund Freud*, Vol. 5, London, Hogarth, 1953, pages 535–536.

———, "Moses and Monotheism," *The Standard Edition of the Complete Psychological Works of Sigmund Freud,* Vol. 23, 1964b, London, Hogarth, page 99.

———, "The Question of Lay Analysis," *The Standard Edition of the Complete Psychological Works of Sigmund Freud,* Vol. 20, 1926, London, Hogarth, page 248.

———, "Three Essays on the Theory of Sexuality," *The Standard Edition of the Complete Psychological Works of Sigmund Freud*, Vol. 7, London, Hogarth, 1955b, pages 125–248.

Interview with Leonardo Gorostiza, "The Lacanian Orientation—*Clarifying the Abruptness of the Real*," *Scríobh*, #7, May 2020, page 3.

Kimon de Greef and Sewell Chan, "Trump Comments, Infuriating Africans, May Set Back U.S. Interests," *New York Times*, January 15, 2018.

Umair Haque, "The Rise of the American Idiot: Why the Rest of the World Doesn't Know Whether to Be Baffled, Horrified, or Dumbstruck by America Right Now," published online at Eudaimonia and Co. Accessed at https://eand.co/the-rise-of-the-american-idiot-dd6c85c445ba on December 27, 2022.

Michael Hardt and Antonio Negri, *Empire*, Cambridge, Harvard University Press, 2001.

Richard Hofstadter, "The Paranoid Style in American Politics," Harper's, November 1964, accessed at https://harpers.org/archive/1964/11/the-paranoid-style-in-american-politics/ on December 28, 2022.

Tom Holland, *Dominion: The Making of the Western World*, London, Little, Brown, 2009.

J. Donald Hughes and J. V. Thirgood. "Deforestation, Erosion, and Forest Management in Ancient Greece and Rome." *Journal of Forest History*. Vol. 26, No. 2. April 1982, pages 60–75.

Claudia Iddan, "Are There Judges?" *Lacanian Review Online*, #103, November 11, 2018, accessed on December 28, 2022, at http://www.thelacanianreviews.com/are-there-judges/

Fredric Jameson, "The Aesthetics of Singularity," *New Left Review*, 92, March–April 2015, pages 101–132.

———, *Archaeologies of the Future: The Desire Called Utopia and Other Science Fictions*, London, Verso, 2007.

———, *Marxism and Form: Twentieth-Century Dialectical Theories of Literature*, Princeton, Princeton University Press, 1971.

———, *The Political Unconscious: Narrative as a Socially Symbolic Act*, Ithaca, Cornell University Press, 1984a.

———, "Postmodernism; or, the Cultural Logic of Late Capitalism" New *Left Review*, 146, July–August 1984b, pages 53–92.

———, *Postmodernism, or, the Cultural Logic of Late Capitalism*, Durham, Duke University Press, 1991.

Immanuel Kant, *"Towards Perpetual Peace" and Other Writings on Politics, Peace, and History*, New Haven, Yale University Press, 2006.

Ibram X. Kendi, *How to Be an Antiracist*, New York, One World, 2019.

Jacques Lacan, "British Psychiatry and the War," *Psychoanalytic Notebooks*, #33 [*The Real and the Social Bond*], June 2019a, pages 11–58.

———, "Du discourse psychanalytique: Discours de Jacques Lacan à l'Université de Milan le 12 mai 1972," *Lacan in Italia 1953–1978: En Italie Lacan*, G. Contri, editor, La Salamandra, 1978, pages 32–55.

———, *Écrits: The First Complete Edition in English*, New York, Norton, 2006a.

———, "Homage to Marguerite Duras, on *Le ravissement de Lol V. Stein,*" *Duras by Duras*, San Francisco, City Light Books, 1987, pages 123–124.

———, "The Neurotic's Individual Myth," *Psychoanalytical Quarterly*, Vol. 48, Issue 3, 1970a, pages 405–425.

———, "Proposition of 9 October 1967a on the Psychoanalyst of the School," accessed on November 19, 2022, at https://lacancircle.com.au/wpcontent/uploads/2017/11/Proposition_of_9_October.pdf.

———, "Radiophonie," *Scilicet*, 2/3, Paris, Seuil, 1970b, pp. 55–99.

———, *The Seminar of Jacques Lacan: Book I, Freud's Papers on Technique (1953–1954),* New York, Norton, 1988a.

———, *The Seminar of Jacques Lacan: Book II: The Ego in Freud's Theory and in the Technique of Psychoanalysis*, W. W. Norton, 1988b.

———, *The Seminar of Jacques Lacan: Book VII, The Ethics of Psychoanalysis, 1959–1960*, New York, Norton, 1992.

———, *The Seminar of Jacques Lacan: Book X: Anxiety (1962–1963),* Cambridge, Polity, 2014.

———, *The Seminar of Jacques Lacan: Book XI: The Four Fundamental Concepts of Psychoanalysis (1963–1964)*, New York, Norton, 1977.

———, *The Seminar of Jacques Lacan: Book XIV: The Logic of Fantasy* (1966–1967). Unpublished translation by Cormac Gallagher. Session of May 10, 1967b. Accessed on October 24, 2022, at http://www.lacaninireland.com/web/wp-content/uploads/2010/06/14-Logic-of-Phantasy-Complete.pdf.

———, *Le séminaire Livre XVI: D'un Autre à l'autre*, Paris, Seuil, 2006b.
———, *The Seminar of Jacques Lacan: Book XVII: The Other Side of Psychoanalysis (1969–1970)*, New York, Norton, 2007.
———, *The Seminar of Jacques Lacan: Book XIX: . . . or Worse (1971–1972)*, Cambridge, Polity, 2018.
———, *The Seminar of Jacques Lacan: Book XX: Encore (1972–1973)*, New York, W. W. Norton, 1998.
———, The Seminar of Jacques Lacan*: Book XXII: RSI (1974–1975)*, unpublished.
———, *The Seminar of Jacques Lacan: Book XXIII: The Sinthome (1975–1976)*, Cambridge, Polity, 2016.
———, *The Seminar of Jacques Lacan: Book XXIV: L'insu que sait de l'une bévue, s'aile à mourre* (1976–1977).
———, *Television: A Challenge to the Psychoanalytic Establishment*, Norton, 1990.
———, "The Third." *The Lacanian Review*, Issue 7, Spring 2019b, Page 104.
Éric Laurent, "The Dialogue Lacan-Kojeve on Bureaucracy and on Empire" on the website of the World Association of Psychoanalysis at https://wapol.org/ornicar/articles/lrn0023.htm, accessed on December 27, 2022a.
———, "Racism 2.0," published online on the *AMP Blog* on January 29, 2014. Accessed at http://ampblog2006.blogspot.com/2014/01/lq-in-english-racism-20-by-eric-laurent.html on December 27, 2022b.
———, "The Real and the Group," *Psychoanalytic Notebooks*, #33, [*The Real and the Social Bond*], June 2019, pages 59–86.
———, "Symptom and Discourse," in *Jacques Lacan and the Other Side of Psychoanalysis: Reflections on Seminar XVII*, Justin Clemens and Russell Grigg, editors, Durham, Duke University Press, 2006, pages 229–253.
———, "The Unconscious and the Body Event," *The Lacanian Review*, #1, Spring 2016, page 181.
Jacques-Alain Miller, "AMP 2008: The Object *a* in the Analytic Experience," *Lacanian Compass*, #1:9, January 5, 2007, pages 4–9.
———, *Analysis Laid Bare*, New York, Lacanian Press, 2023.
———, "Extimité" in *Lacanian Theory of Discourse: Subject, Structure and Society*, New York, New York University Press, 1988, pages 74–87.
———, "A Fantasy" *Lacanian Praxis: International Quarterly of Applied Psychoanalysis*, #1, 2005, page 15.
———, "Histoires de . . . psychanalyse" at https://www.lacan.com/millerlecture.htm, accessed on December 28, 2020.

———, "Milanese Intuitions [1]," *Mental Online: International Journal of Mental Health and Applied Psychoanalysis*, #11, December 2002, pages 9–16.
———, "Milanese Intuitions [2]," *Mental Online: International Journal of Mental Health and Applied Psychoanalysis*, #12, May 2003, page 10.
———, "On Shame," in *Jacques Lacan and the Other Side of Psychoanalysis: Reflections on Seminar XVII, Op. cit.*
———. "The Real for the 21st Century." In World Association of Psychoanalysis (Eds.). *Scilicet: A Real for the 21st Century*, Paris, NLS Publication, 2014, pages 25–36.
———, "The Real Unconscious," *The Lacanian Review*, 6, Fall 2018a, pages 29–46.
———, "Six Paradigms of Jouissance," *Psychoanalytical Notebooks*, 34, December 2019, pages 11–80.
———, "The Space of a Hallucination," *The Lacanian Review*, #6, Fall 2018b, page 82–108.
———, "The Space of a Lapsus," *The Lacanian Review*, #6, Fall 2018c, page 62–81.
———, "Les Trumains," accessed online October 13, 2022, at https://congresoamp2020.com/en/articulos.php?sec=el-tema&sub=textos-de-orientacion&file=el-tema/textos-de-orientacion/20-03-02_los-trumanos.html&utm_source=Campa.
———, "We Love the One Who Responds to Our Question: 'Who Am I?" *Psychologies Magazine*, Issue 278, October 2008.
Catherine Millet, *The Sexual Life of Catherine M.*, New York, Grove, 2002.
Timothy Morton, *Hyperobjects: Philosophy and Ecology after the End of the World*, Minneapolis, University of Minnesota Press, 2013.
Barack Obama and David Simon. "A Conversation with President Obama and The Wire Creator David Simon" on the the "Obama White House" YouTube site. Accessed at https://www.youtube.com/watch?v=xWY79JCfhjw on April 3, 2022.
Mark O'Connell. "What Are the Plastic Particles in Our Bodies Doing to Us." *The New York Times*. April 23, 2023. Page SR6.
Elvis Presley, Lyrics, "A Little Less Conversation," accessed on Google lyrics search on January 16, 2024.
Arthur Rimbaud, *Rimbaud: Complete Works, Selected Letters*, Chicago, University of Chicago Press, 1966, page 304.
Kim Stanley Robinson, *The Ministry for the Future*, New York, Orbit/Hachette Book Group, 2020.

Joshua Rothman, "Can Science Fiction Wake Us Up to Our Climate Reality? Kim Stanley Robinson's novels envision the dire problems of the future—but also their solutions," *The New Yorker*, January 24, 2022, page 34.
John Schwartz, "Where's Airborne Plastic? Everywhere, Scientists Find: There's "no nook or cranny" on the planet where it doesn't end up, the lead researcher on a new study said." *The New York Times*, June 11, 2020, accessed at https://www.nytimes.com/2020/06/11/climate/airborne-plastic-pollution.html?searchResultPosition=8 on December 27, 2023.
"South Omaha Mob Wars on the Greeks," *New York Times*, Feb 22, 1909, page 1.
Bruce Springsteen, *Born to Run*, New York, Simon & Schuster, 2016.
Nidhi Subbaraman. "Pacific Ocean Garbage Patch Is Bursting With Life." *Wall Street Journal*, April 17, 2023.
Thomas Svolos, *The Aims of Analysis: Miami Seminar on the Late Lacan*, New York, Midden Press, 2020.
———, "Coronavirus and the Hole in the Big Other," *Letters in Quarantine: Psychoanalytic Chronicles of a Pandemic*, Florencia F.C. Shanahan with Marie-Hélène Brousse and Cyrus Saint Amand Poliakoff, editors, New York, Lacanian Press, 2021a, pages 443–445.
———, "História e a conexão do ato analítico com a civilização" in *Boletim Travessias* [electronic journal of the Escola Brasileira de Psicanálise] #5. Accessed October 27, 2021b, at https://ebp.org.br/sp/historia-e-a-conexao-do-ato-analitico-com-a-civilizacao/
———, "Psychoanalysis and Politics: Duane Rousselle Interviews Thomas Svolos, " in the Salon section of the e-journal European Journal of Psychoanalysis] on Nov 3, 2022. Accessed at https://www.journal-psychoanalysis.eu/articles/psychoanalysis-and-politics-duane-rouselle-interviews-thomas-svolos/ on December 27, 2023.
———, *Twenty-First Century Psychoanalysis*, London, Karnac, 2017.
Jakob von Uexküll, *A Foray into the Worlds of Animals and Humans: with A Theory of Meaning*, Minneapolis, University of Minnesota Press, 2010.
Yannis Varoufakis, *Adults in the Room: My Battle with the European and American Deep Establishment*, Farrar, Straus, and Giroux, 2017.
The West Wing
Wikipedia, https://en.wikipedia.org/wiki/Anti-Greek_sentiment and also
———, https://en.wikipedia.org/wiki/Black_Lives_Matter
———, https://en.wikipedia.org/wiki/Canuck_letter
———, https://en.wikipedia.org/wiki/Don%27t_Look_Up

———, https://en.wikipedia.org/wiki/Greek_Town_riot
———, https://en.wikipedia.org/wiki/Hyperobject_Industries
———, https://en.wikipedia.org/wiki/Omaha_race_riot_of_1919
Slavoj Zizek, *The Sublime Object of Ideology*, London, Verso, 1989.

Index[1]

[1] Note: Page numbers followed by 'n' refer to notes.

T. Svolos, *Culture and Politics on the Couch*, The Palgrave Lacan Series,
https://doi.org/10.1007/978-3-031-61365-4

The manufacturer's authorised representative in the EU is Springer Nature Customer Service Centre GmbH, Europaplatz 3, 69115 Heidelberg, Germany. If you have any concerns regarding our products, please contact ProductSafety@springernature.com

Printed and bound by CPI Group (UK) Ltd, Croydon, CR0 4YY
28/09/2026
02224083-0010